Acupuncture
for Your Soul

A Collection of Life-Changing *Aha!* Moments

Rae Jacob

Acupuncture for Your Soul: A Collection of Life-Changing Aha! Moments

Copyright © 2016 Rae Jacob. All rights reserved. No part of this book may be reproduced or retransmitted in any form or by any means without the written permission of the publisher.

Published by Wheatmark®
1760 East River Road, Suite 145
Tucson, Arizona 85718 USA
www.wheatmark.com

ISBN: 978-1-62787-340-6 (paperback)
ISBN: 978-1-62787-341-3 (ebook)
LCCN: 2015956646

This adventure, this book is dedicated to
my best friend, my husband, Danny Jacob, Sr.
and
The Sisters of the Guam Carmelite Monastery

You know what the issue is with this world?
Everyone wants some magical solution to their
problem and everyone refuses to believe in magic.

The Mad Hatter, *Alice's Adventure in Wonderland* by Lewis Carroll

What's Inside

CELEBRATING ACUPUNCTURE FOR YOUR SOUL MOMENTS

YOUR ACUPUNCTURE FOR YOUR SOUL PAGES

Acupuncture (Latin,'acus' (needle) 'punctura' (to puncture) is a form of alternative medicine and a key component of Traditional Chinese Medicine (TCM) involving the stimulation of specific acupuncture points along the skin of the body using thin needles. According to TCM, this process is believed to adjust and alter the body's energy flow (chi) into healthier patterns that strengthen the body and prompt it to heal itself.

At the core of acupuncture is spiritual transformation.

—Sara Calabro

Foreword

I have known Rae Jacob my entire life. As she celebrates 80 years on this earth, I marvel at her and the effect she has on every living soul she encounters.

There are not many hidden parts to Rae. She is definitely WYSIWYG (What You See Is What You Get).

Her winning combination is what I like to call her "simplistic complexities." She has always been a God-centered, loving person, refusing to see the negative which can creep into one's life and draw down the positive spirit of a soul.

Once you meet Rae (and you don't even have to meet her in person,) a simple joyful energy finds it's way into your soul, leaving you to wonder, "Why do I feel so utterly peaceful and happy?"

Then, even if for a moment, you begin to understand the world as if you are Rae! This is where the complexities begin.

Once touched by this notion of genuine, God-Centered happiness, you go out and affect someone else—close or even not so close—to you. Then they impact someone else. And on and on it goes. Before you know it, there is this underlying current of thousands of souls connected by light and energy, leading back to Rae.

Suddenly, all of the grace and goodness you once felt from Rae, has expanded, unknowingly to the rest of the universe. The ripple effect of this light energy is, I believe, the invisible golden thread that ties everyone together in her first published book, "Acupuncture for Your Soul."

As you will find, Rae was given a message, which I believe came from her best friends, The Choir of Angels—the same Choir of Angels that has guided her and her family throughout the course of her life. This was an unusually strong message. For in a very short time, Rae, a self-proclaimed positive procrastinator, gathered these stories and created the book you are reading right now.

The most amazing aspect of this venture is that the stories are from men and women from many spectrums of life, different races and ages, with a variety of spiritual beliefs, some of whom have suffered greatly, some of whom have suffered little, some who are rich, some who are poor, some that are her children, and many that feel as though they are her children. She has achieved, albeit on a smaller scale, what governments, religions, and special interests groups can only dream about —inclusivity.

Only the simplistic God-Centered nature of Rae

could have brought forth these stories from these individuals simply by asking that they participate. Her request sparked a powerful chain reaction of inspiration. The stories that all of these individuals prepared themselves to share with the world come from a deep and authentic spiritual place. They are here to awaken and resonate with your own deep and authentic spiritual place.

On a deeply personally note, I must add that one of the greatest gifts that Rae has given me, is the ability to SEE. From a young age, she taught me how to see the physical world. To paint it, draw it, and build it. Within the metaphysical world, she taught me how to see through the eyes of my intuition. As much as I sometimes try to ignore my spiritual gifts, it is an impossibility. When I close my eyes to sleep or meditate, I start to see the colors of my day—my worries and my future. All of those colors slowly turn into the simple golden strand that leads back to Rae Jacob, my own Mother.

Thank you for writing this book and thank you for showing all of us that no matter what, anything is possible.

Your loving son, Randy

Randel William Jacob, Architect, NCARB

Introduction

The Very First Acupuncture for your Soul

It was at mass in the grace-filled Carmelite chapel in Guam that I was overcome with this incredible peace, the one we read and hear about, the one beyond all understanding. This was the peace I tasted, felt, and swam in for precious moments.

The words, rich with feeling, flashed in front of me: This is *Acupuncture for your Soul.* The day before I had received acupuncture for my legs. The result was amazing. My body experienced a great flow of circulation and freedom from discomfort—such release. A relief from focusing on what did not feel comfortable. During those precious moments in the chapel I felt the same comfort, flow, release in my soul.

It was a giant hug of unconditional love. A spark of God—become almost visible, conveying: "Everything in your life is in perfect Divine Order."

Acupuncture for your Soul, I thought. Could this be the title of a book? The intention was set.

Been a long time since that morning in Guam in 2009. Over the last several years due to health circumstances and Spirit, I have been gifted with what I call "re-wirings." There has been abundant opportunity to just "BE." I've been told many times through the years that I needed to slow down and learn to be "a human BEING and not just a human DOING!" Hmmm, when I was young that did not appeal at all.

But then I am old now (chronologically old) and grateful for "the spiritual opportunity of illness," a quote from my friend, Jane Hermes, who lived a life full of family, laughter, buoyant spirit and suffering. Jane had an eye removed due to cancer. Her comment? "Ok, I have another one." When told she had liver cancer and would be dead in two months, she laughed at the doctor. "Don't worry, Dear, only God knows when I will die." She was and still is an inspiration, an acupuncture for my soul in the form of a friend, who enriched my life.

With encouragement from her and many spiritual teachers, I've discovered that "being" is really a fertile space to inhabit. It is comfortable, even delicious to have had so much personal solitude these last years. How grateful and blessed I feel to have had this time to clear the clutter from the physical, emotional, mental, spiritual closets of my life. An ongoing process. One of meeting myself, remembering who I am, who I was, who I am becoming.

As Danielle LaPorte says, "Who were you before the world told you who to be?"

Uncovering the answer has been and is for me a

fun, adventurous and surprising ACUPUNCTURE FOR MY SOUL journey!

It fueled me with the desire to inspire acupuncture for your soul moments in others.

And so, this book.

In this offering of Aha! Moments from people of various backgrounds, ages, and spiritual beliefs, some stories will resonate immediately. Others may awaken something within you more slowly. No matter, the right voice at the right time can open your heart and guide you into a deeper, richer life, step by step or all at once.

Surely you will be as moved and humbled as I am by the authentic stories our writers have shared with us.

Why would they do this?
Why would they expose their souls?
Why are they sharing their Aha! Moments,
Their dark nights of the soul,
Their life-changing experiences?

It is a gift of uplifting, amazing moments,
of connection—
to know that whatever we feel,
Whatever our personal experience may be that
we are not alone!

We are all interconnected—
check out quantum physics!

The purpose of these heartfelt, honest stories
is to offer—

empowerment,
encouragement,
consolation,
inspiration,
laughter,
love,
and ideally the motivation, courage, and
sanctuary to recognize, be with, honor, and
write your own life-changing experiences,

Your own **Acupuncture for your soul!**
What are your Aha! Moments?

Play with the blank *Acupuncture for Your Soul*
pages in the back of the book. Empower yourself by
acknowledging your life experiences. Remember the
incidents that remain hidden are the ones that usurp
our life force.

Dive into your own lives.
Let it be an adventure.
No one is judging you.
Make it a Light exercise.
YOU *have so much to share!*

Love and Hugs,

Rae

Acupuncture for Your Soul Begins

The beautiful trials, tribulations and even triumphs in our lives can block or clog our energy and diminish our life force. When we acknowledge what is going on with us, what we have experienced or are experiencing, we can begin to free ourselves from pain and fear and open the contracted areas of our Soul.

—Soonalyn Jacob

There is no greater agony in life than bearing an untold story inside of you.

—Maya Angelou

In other words, *Acupuncture (for your soul)*

releases

the flow of chi / lifeforce / energy

to strengthen

balance

and

allow

life-changing

explorations

expansions &

experiences.

Aha! Moments of life

Release,

revive,

rejuvenate!

Longing for the Light

KIMBERLY JACOB

I woke up in the neuro-intensive care unit with my neurosurgeon and his team of residents staring at me in their white coats.

"Where were you?" the surgeon asked. "You were gone a long time. We've been waiting for you to come back." He smiled compassionately.

I just closed my eyes. I couldn't tell him where I had been. It became clearer as the next few weeks passed by. How could I ever put it into words? I knew I had just been to Heaven and seen the face of God. I had felt unconditional, peaceful love and stood among the most glorious light I had ever felt. I witnessed the power and love of God and was so overwhelmed and joyful. Then I was suddenly pulled back. I knew somewhere in my mind that I should be grateful that I had just survived brain surgery, but I wasn't.

My friends and family kept telling me how blessed I was but I didn't feel it. I felt disappointed, a little angry and very confused. I wanted to go back. I wanted to be there, not here. The feelings lingered but I kept them to myself. I wanted to go home. The next many, many months I tried to convince myself otherwise.

It had all happened so fast. I was a physical therapist on a neurological rehabilitation unit at one of the best Neurological Institutes in the world. I had loved my work and the people I worked with. We were a family. It was special. I was exactly where I wanted to be. And I was good at what I did. I worked with patients from all over the world who came for brain surgery. I would come in early, leave late and not even recognize that the day was done. The brain and its ability to heal fascinated me. Neuroplasticity of the brain is more efficient with proper rehabilitation. Helping patients get there was my heaven on earth. Most of my patients could not verbalize, but we always found a way to communicate through touch, tears, laughter, anger, hugs, fear, and joy. We worked very, very hard to make what sometimes seemed like a tiny bit of progress. Each tiny bit became a small piece that eventually became a big piece of their puzzle. It was an honor, a blessing, and a privilege to be part of their very personal yet, extraordinary miracle. I dreamed of going to medical school and started to study for the MCAT exam. Life was good.

My dear friend and co-worker, Tony, encouraged me to see a neurologist after hearing me complain of recurring headaches and changes in my vision. I thought he was being overprotective. I pushed it aside until the day he dialed up the doctor and handed me the phone to make the appointment.

Sitting with the doctor at the appointment, I instinctively knew that something wasn't right. I would not leave the room until he gave me a prescription to get an MRI, which I scheduled that day. The next day I found myself face to face with the neurologist, neuro-oncologist and neurosurgeon who all told me I had a mass in my brain and it had to come out ASAP!

I asked each of them the same question: "Are you sure you are looking at the MRI of MY brain??"

The neurosurgeon, who I admired and respected so much and whose patients I had treated, asked if I had any questions.

"Yes," I said. "I treat a lot of your patients and I just want to know—what am I going to look like?

And," I asked again. "Are you sure you are looking at the right scan? I am fine. I went to work today and look at me. Nothing is wrong!"

The denial began right there. He confirmed who I was and finally took me to see for myself. As I stood in a large open area with a long wall lined with bright light X-ray readers, he showed me the walnut-sized tumor in the frontal parietal area of my right brain.

He put his hand on my shoulder, looked at me and said, "You will be fine. Maybe a little weak on your left side, but it is contained and I can easily go in and scoop it out."

I believed him. That is the moment my healing began. I trusted him. He was compassionate and understanding.

He then announced that he wanted to take out the tumor in the morning.

"What!" I said. "Tonight is Valentine's Day and I have a date AND I have other plans for the weekend! No way tomorrow I am having brain surgery!"

"Okay," he said. "But no later than Monday."

So it was. I reportedly did well following surgery. I stayed in ICU for a day, then was moved to the neuro floor of the hospital where I had worked closely with the staff for the past many years. I had another few scans, a physical therapy evaluation and many other blood draws, visitors and tests. I do not remember much of it.

That night, my mom stayed in the hospital room with me and apparently kept ringing for the nurse most of the time. She believed something was wrong. It wasn't until 5 the next morning when my sister Beth, who is a nurse, came to say goodbye, that people took notice. My sister took one look at me and told my mom to get in the hall and scream for help. It was no accident that one of my doctor friends was doing her rounds early that morning. She came running and got me back to surgery to excavate blood that had bled out from the tumor bed.

What happened next was amazing. I had fallen into a coma and felt myself moving in a tunnel toward a peaceful, quiet, yet brilliant light. It was the kind of light that is nonexistent on earth. The kind of light that you would never need to squint your eyes at. The kind of light that penetrated through me and stayed with me as if I was the light. I did not have to do anything to receive this light and love. I did not have to give anything to be in this light. This was the touch and embrace of God. I could rest like I never have rested before. Or since.

I made it through the tunnel and was at the edge of this beautiful light energy. I could see other forms of light with a large form of this LOVE in the middle.

I reached with all my inner being to become one with this light. Just as it was about to merge with me...I was pulled back! I was angry, sad, confused and upset. I learned weeks later, when retelling this to my mom, that at that time she and the world were praying for me not to die. The magnetic POWER OF PRAYER pulled me back.

Over the next many months, I became clinically depressed. I had support, but I could not pull myself back to here. I was changed forever. Yet I wore myself out trying to fit into who I was before. Who I was supposed to be. I was tormented.

I can say that to this day I still have a deep sadness around this. Don't get me wrong. I don't have a death wish. But I will embrace the time when I really go back to this peaceful, loving light. I am no longer afraid to leave this earth. I am no longer scared when loved ones die. I KNOW they are THERE. After this experience, I now KNOW that we are all connected and we are connected by only one thing: LOVE.

There are glimpses of this love and light on earth but they are only sparks that last only as long as fireworks on 4th of July or a sparkler that burns out before it is supposed to.

I am close to this light when I practice daily meditation. I am close to this light when I am with children who are still part way in Heaven and haven't learned all there is to be a being on this earth. They are joy to me. I am close to this light when I can comfort or assist in the healing of another person through intention, touch or healing modalities. I am here to do this work. I am a healer and I am powered by the light and love of God. These things I know.

What I don't know is exactly how this will play out over the rest of my life. There are many pieces to this story that are sad for me still. The passion and love I had for my work with people that had been victims of neurological insult is gone. How could this be? I tried and tried to find it. Maybe it was the setting? I changed settings. Perhaps the problem was that I was working in the same hospital on the same floors with the same doctors that treated me. I wasn't sure if I was supposed to jump in bed with my patients or run as far away as I could! I understood too closely what they were feeling. I tried to soothe myself by telling myself that I was lucky, that I wasn't as bad off as they were, that I could walk, talk , etc.

The denial and inability to accept what was going on only took me farther and farther from my soul. I had multiple medical shocks to my body. A hysterectomy and the grief that comes from not bearing a child, a removal of a kidney from cancer, orthopedic surgeries, and other surgeries on my head. I was depressed and in denial for almost 20 years before

I had the courage to quit that work and pursue another softer form of healing. When I quit my job, the physical illnesses stopped. Not a coincidence! So my "Aha!" Moment is yet to come. I feel that it will come as I follow my soul's path with 100 percent conviction. Okay, even 80 percent conviction. But I am not there yet.

If I was there, then perhaps I would not be here?

Kimberly Jacob *is owner of Integrative Physical Therapy and Wellness, LLC (www.integrativetherapywellness. com).Her practice brings together 30 years as a Neurological Physical Therapist at Barrow Neurological Institute and a variety of community, home, school, and private settings. She currently focuses on assisting her clients to ENGAGE IN LIFE and move into wholeness through a variety of modalities including: Functional mobility, safety assessment, strength and endurance training for clients in their homes. Kimberly adds Craniosacral Therapy, Myofascial Release, meditation, breath techniques and aromatherapy to her toolbox. Kimberly has a passion to teach Meditation/Contemplative prayer to young children. She believes that this will change our world one little soul at a time! She lives in Phoenix, AZ with her husband Paul and son Morgan. She is available for workshops, lectures and private sessions.*

Kari Strand

Life Paid Forward:
An Improvisation

ANN HAMPTON CALLAWAY

Tonight as stars
Become the leaves of bare trees
And the moon becomes
A knowing smile,
I river back to times of
Skies cleared within.
At four, a Sunday school lesson
Of the Golden Rule

Setting me on course—Its pure soul logic
Ringing me true
And readying compassion
As my vehicle of time.
At eight, learning
The Optimist's Creed
On my grandmother's knee-
Reciting and discussing each line
Till there were rays around me
Like a sun.
Those rays helped me when
My very same grandmother
Took her life two years later.
At nine, reading Andre Gide
From my father's bookshelf—
"Art is the collaboration
Between God and the artist
And the less the artist does, the better."
I'm still trying to do less.
At twelve, reading Bob Dylan's
Free association book "Tarantula"
And deciding to journal and let words
Somersault out to surprise me
With what I didn't know I knew.
At thirteen, reading "Autobiography of a Yogi"
And learning what human beings
Are capable of spiritually,

Confirming a lifelong hunch.
At fourteen, creating "Greatness Training"
Summer courses for myself
By regular trips to the library to
See great art, hear great music and
Read great literature, hoping my mind
Would develop tools
To enter new portals.
At seventeen, asking my English teacher,
"Mrs. Pink, how I could possibly write anything
Since all the great ideas had been written?"
And hearing her say, "No one has ever
Lived your life before. Write about that."
At twenty, after being ravaged by small minded
And bitter teachers in college,
Auditioning with fifteen of my friends,
Including my sister, for CCM Musical Theater
Program And everybody getting in but me,
Learning how passionate I was about my dreams
And deciding to move to New York
To create my own education.
Fast forward to thirty three
And meeting the spiritual teacher
I'd always yearned for-
The Master of meditation
Who woke up all the light in me
From her great light,

Giving me the tools
For a relationship with God
As experienced in all things, all people,
All times and all places.
Tonight, I bow to her and to
So many lessons, so many stars,
So many clouds lifted by gestures,
Conversations, and pure energy
Like the energy of our radiant friend,
Who felt my depletion from a joyous
But stressful life,
And laid me down to rest with healing
Energy, lifesaving my wheels of being.
To these rainbowed moments
I give thanks, anchored in the understanding
That gratitude is how the will to live
Makes its majestic arabesque
Each day. Yes, to all my teachers and healers,
May my life pay forward
What you have given me
In the currency of what this is all about:
Love.

As a creative spirit inspired by a rich spiritual life, **Ann Hampton Callaway** *has made her mark as a singer, pianist, composer, lyricist, arranger, actress, educator, TV host and producer. She won the Theater World Award and received a Tony nomination for her starring role in the Broadway musical "Swing!" She's written over 250 songs including two Platinum Award winning hits for Barbra Streisand and the theme for the hit TV series "The Nanny." Ann has recorded 12 solo CD's including her newest "From Sassy to Divine: The Sarah Vaughan Project" and is a guest artist on over 50 CD's. You can find her at: www.annhamptoncallaway.com. To learn more about her spiritual inspiration, visit: www.siddhayoga.org.*

The Third Mary

ROSLYN ELENA McGRATH

"No, I don't want to!" I exclaimed. It was a skill I'd developed over a lifetime or more, the ability to verbalize a clear, unequivocal line between what I would and would not do, and to stand firm on it, a skill that had kept confusion, risks and crash landings at bay. But this time, it accomplished nothing but to reveal a smidgen of the emotional charge I felt. I began to receive the other-dimensional communication anyway.

I was not "born with the lights on," seeing and speaking with angels and beings who'd passed over from birth. I'd experienced some déjà vu and even occasional precognition for food (another story!) while growing up, and I can now look back and recognize other instances of intuition at work, but it wasn't until a health challenge catalyzed my conscious spiritual journey that I began to deliberately "tune in."

Over time, my intuition, (aided by practices I'd learned and my choice to develop it), became an increasingly regular, supportive resource in my everyday world. The more I used this ability, the stronger it became. It offers me insights into others' challenges and personal messages from spiritual teachers, guides, angels, and loved ones on the other side, to support achieving breakthroughs.

So when I first read *I Remember Union*, a retelling of Mary Magdalene's role as integral and vital to Jesus's mission, written by Flo Aeveia Magdalena, it was not unusual for me to feel echoes of something more than the printed words themselves. I resonated deeply with this book, reading it three times over a 7 year period, each instance bringing me a new and meaningful experience of the story. Yet one element remained consistent. Each time I read this revision of Mary Magdalene's part in Biblical times, I would hear, "And you were her mother."

Now, I take such messages with several large grains of salt. After all, aren't we all one, ultimately? Add to that the cellular memory of our genetic structure, which may allow us to tap into ancestral memories. And also consider the concept related in *I Remember Union* that those of us alive now may carry aspects of souls who played larger-than-life roles in Biblical times.

Be that as it may, though Mary Magdalene's mother is mentioned only briefly in *I Remember Union*, the emotion I felt regarding my connection with her was so intense, it seemed it might completely engulf me. I carried this secret within me, believing I should not share it or look at it. So when I felt pushed to reveal it to a close friend who is also deeply affected by I Remember Union, and she strongly suggested I dialogue with this being to uncover her story, I did not want to go there.

But apparently it was too late. As soon as the suggestion was given, I began to hear the voice of Mary Magdalene's mother in the background of my mind. Early the next morning, while I was still half-asleep, she told me very clearly:

I was the one who showed her how to send.
I was the one who showed her how to send.
I was the one who told her not to bend.
I was the one who told her not to bend.

I was the one who showed her love has no end.
Love has no end.
Love has no end.[1]

She also shared the following with me:

What else could I do but what I had to? I knew she (Mary Magdalene) would absolve all wrongs, mend them at a level that I never

1   Roslyn Elena McGrath, The Third Mary: 55 Messages for Empowering Truth, Peace &Grace from the Mother of Mary Magdalene (Michigan: Chrysaetos Press, 2014), 1.

knew. I also knew the cost, and that my job was never to judge her for choosing a road so hard, though it broke my heart thousands of times over. I thank her for changing the world, and challenging me to love through the pain, through the hardship of one who knows the bitter taste of sacrifice for long term, all-worlds gain. The energy was so heavy then. You would not recognize your world. You think it is difficult now with suicides, drug addictions, plagues. Our times were more brutal, mercy far less common, our thirst for Heaven more prevalent because of this.

I know you have to go now. I will write with you again. My story must be told. I thank you.

La Magdalena[2]

I wrote these words down, and about a week later committed to taking down the messages she chose to share with me. This culminated in my publishing *The Third Mary: 55 Messages for Empowering Truth, Peace &Grace from the Mother of Mary Magdalene,* a book which weaves stories of the past, present and future with parables, insights and advice for greater peace

---

2   Ibid., 3.

and self-empowerment, a book whose creation and sharing deeply fulfills me.

The day I made this commitment, the Third Mary (Mary Magdalene's mother) explained that I found her "heavy within myself" because I was "responding very emotionally to the Heart of the Truth," and also because of unresolved emotional wounds from Biblical times.

It wasn't long, however, before I looked forward to taking down her messages as the best part of my day, rich with meaning and purpose. Though I have focused on what is truly worth doing with my life for the past twenty years, this activity brought a whole new level of purposefulness to me. And the intense emotion regarding my connection with the Third Mary had dissolved.

Just as important to me as the messages within the book itself, and perhaps as an example of the potential of their teachings, my communication with the Third Mary has brought me a strength, a knowing, a groundedness, stability and confidence beyond what I experienced in my life prior to this. For example, when I make a seemingly "big" life choice, such as investing a considerable amount of money to go on a Mary Magdalene-focused tour of France, I don't repeatedly review my decision. Nor do I question the value of my work, or the appropriateness of taking care of my personal needs.

More of me is here now, as well as the constant availability of the Third Mary's wise and helpful presence in a way that is more tangible to me than other spiritual beings I have channeled. I am so very grateful to be able to share from my heart some of her power through my life, in ways both just begun and yet to unfold.

Roslyn Elena McGrath continues learning to channel herself fully into her multi-faceted vocation of creating and sharing Empowering Lightworks—energy, insights, and inspiration to shine your light in the many ways and forms in which they reveal themselves to her. Her love of food, friends, family and nature roots her creative spirit. She lives with her beloved husband and cockapoo along the shores of Lake Superior in beautiful Marquette, MI. To discover more, go to: www.EmpowermentLightworks.com and www.ThirdMary.com.

The Divine Mother is dancing with us,

dancing within us.

She wants us

to be aware and

to enjoy ourselves

in our dance with Her.

As we do so

we take our place

as another conscious part of the Whole,

dancing with every other part,

dancing within every other part.

Please

dance

with

us.

—Sarahni (Susan) Stumpf

Fire in the Belly

Carol Markham-Cousins

For the past 34 years I have worked in education with a fire in my belly to be the voice of all students.

The Minneapolis Public School District recruited me to come to Washburn High to turn around a failing school that had a disproportionate number of poor black students not achieving. A turnaround would take time, vision and hard work. I, as principal, tirelessly spent the first two years in the homes of the people around Washburn talking about the risks, the innovation, the passion and commitment needed to make this change. The change happened, we took the bold move to "Fresh Start" this high school, turn over the staff, change the curriculum and build a trusting culture. The school thrived, for all students and neighborhood families began to attend for the first time in 20 years, increasing the enrollment nearly 100 percent.

Beginning in 2013 the district changed the school zoning, and wealthy white families were now not given the option to attend any school of their "choice" in Minneapolis. Washburn High School became the only available public school option for the neighborhood families. Some parents were fearful that the heterogeneous classrooms would not challenge their student.

This is a non-traditional approach of including ALL the 9th and 10th grades students in the humanities courses, without testing or selecting out a group of "higher" performing students. A few influential families expected me to change what we had been developing over the past 5 years. I listened, but refused to make the changes these few powerful parents wanted. It was time to push beyond the status quo and challenge the perceptions of what students could achieve.

Standing up for equity in education in the face of fear and racism changed the course of my career.

Because I refused to change, challenged the district decision to reverse direction and begin tracking students in the humanities and exposed other unethical practices, the leadership took the bold move of removing me as principal 6 weeks before the end of school, without any grace or true explanation.

I believed in my heart that I had done nothing to deserve the disrespect and public humiliation by district officials who pulled me out of the school, reversed support of the innovations that deliberately include all students in rigorous coursework, and remained silent, refusing to counter the misperceptions written about me in the newspaper. Born in the Washburn High School neighborhood, I continued to live within blocks of the school. Stopping in the bakery, running around the lake, attending the YWCA, I faced people who did not know the truth every day. The drastic measure of reassigning me had been more hurtful than anything I had experienced in my 34-year career.

Longing to do the work that I love and be free of the negativity of the past few years, I embarked on the adventure of moving to New York City. As principal in charge of creating a new charter high school in Washington Heights/Inwood, I lived in a diverse community and became part of the largest school district in the country.

Living in one of the greatest cities in the world has given me the opportunity to witness both the best and the worst in education. Racial segregation in NYC is even greater than in Minneapolis, yet New Yorkers are more than willing to talk about race and go to heart of this issue. What I did not realize is that this move would catapult me to an organization that represents some of the worst aspects of our educational system. For example, teacher pay is dependent on student scores on standardized tests and many of the "teachers" were without any license or experience to work with the poorest students in the city. These are just two examples amongst many more blatant and damaging practices.

For the first time, I felt completely alone. I live for relationships, so this was hard for me. But it provided an unexpected gift. Space, time, and distance to look within. After much meditation and reflection, I decided I couldn't stay in New York. I am back in Minneapolis now. At one time my hopes focused primarily on pushing forward, changing injustice, challenging the status quo, gathering support to transform education. Now after many years of taking on challenges and fighting publicly for what I believe in, I am ready to slow down and gather together my spirit. I have the same big dreams but many of my hopes are more internal; I am seeking that wisdom that can come with age and experience.

Meditation through yoga has been an opportunity for me to reflect and ponder. One interesting meditation has been to observe myself first as a spirit, and then a physical body. I have experienced a glimpse of my spirit.

My hope is to continue to reveal to myself what makes up my spirit. And to discover how to "be human" in the midst of physical aging, professional disappointments, environmental inevitabilities, strained or stressed relationships—and live with purpose and joy.

What is the tiny glimpse I have of my spirit? All Voices Do Matter, whether I agree with the words or not. I don't need to be louder. I desire to be even stronger, listen even longer, and try to observe with eyes from behind the words. I have the opportunity every day to make a difference in the lives of whomever I come in contact with, the librarian, waitress, barista, people on the bus, my sons, and my husband. This glimpse is a light that illuminates my humanness in the form of my spirit, not my job, my position, my status, but my strength, passions and desires.

I now have a fire in my soul!

Carol Markham-Cousins has lived and worked as an educator in the Minneapolis metropolitan area her entire life, except for extended travel and a sabbatical in Cuenca, Ecuador. Since the age of 18, she has traveled extensively throughout much of the world, and developed a passion for transforming education in the United States. Being the parent of two amazing young men, and married to the same supportive man for 31 years has provided her with the strength and passion to pursue a 35-year career in education from the classroom to the community. You can find her on: www.linkedin.com.

How I Got out of the Convent

MARTI MATTHEWS

A very slight shift it was, but it put me on a new path that began to diverge away from exterior obedience and increasingly towards hearing and trusting my own inner guide.

I was raised a Roman Catholic, a warm world full of symbols and color and ecstatic images of devotion, love, and noble aspirations. But there were some traps. The idea that had its jaws around me was the teaching called "original sin" and the consequent need for salvation. This belief tells us that as soon as we've taken a breath into the world we are sinful because our ancestors ate an apple when they were told not to; that the almighty creator-of-all required the horrible death of his son to make amends for this; that suffering is a noble way to show our love to this almighty power who is still said to be loving and merciful. The glorification of suffering was the spider web that had me trapped.

For various reasons, by the time I was a teenager, my mind was a mess. I lived in a dual world. During the school year my life was a small farm town high school class of 44 students; I spent summers at a camp for rich city girls, a camp whose mission was to make Christian leaders out of us, champions of great deeds in the world. I felt I was unable to succeed well in either place, but that I did have something to give to the world. I felt most powerful and alive in academics. I loved to learn, and felt especially attracted to subjects like literature, philosophy, theology – instinctively searching for ways to look at life that might help me feel happier. I had not yet discovered psychology, and any self-help books I encountered were based in the Christian trap-story (sacrifice, unselfishness, noble suffering).

My one hope, what attracted me, was to go to a great place of learning—our state university— where I could be challenged academically. With trepidation, I placed the secret longing of my heart before my father. He quickly said, "No. You'd just be a little fish in a big sea. You'll be homesick like my sister was at a big state college." (Though she stayed and finished there!) Thus in an instant my dream was snuffed out. I knew nothing about scholarships. There were no counselors in our high school. There weren't even jobs in our town of 500 people! So now I had to find another path to a future.

I became even more religious, praying for guidance. In those days (the 50s-60s) women did not choose to live unmarried. My dad referred to two single sisters in our extended family as "the old maids," even though they were teachers and had traveled all over the world. Perhaps because neither of my parents had ever seemed happy in their marriage, I did not see myself getting married. I had even less interest in raising children. How to avoid the pressures to get married?

I often heard mention in passing of a holy spirit, the "Holy Ghost," who was said to bring us wisdom and comfort, guidance and courage, but our religious practices did not relate much to this promising presence. Most of our practices emphasized our sinful state and the incredible suffering it took for Jesus to rescue us from this. I thought, "If God is the almighty and loving father, he would help me see a path, like my father would if he could, imperfect as he was." Becoming a nun seemed an option, a possible but unclear path to the academic and service work I longed for. I wasn't thrilled about the idea of wearing odd clothes and being separated from the world that so interested me, but it was a path that would protect me from pressure to marry. Another appealing feature of the convent at that point of my life was giving someone else responsibility to make decisions for me!

I looked over the different orders of nuns and chose one based on their lifestyle, not their work. One goal I had identified for my future was to be a saint. Saints were the best! The path of the saints had been laid out before me as the example par excellence of a person dedicated to doing good. Another trap door? The saints not only did great deeds helping the poor and suffering, but to qualify for sainthood one had to suffer a lot oneself, maybe die for the cause, sacrifice much, be misunderstood and humiliated. If the saints were happy and their lives went smoothly, it was not advertised.

This order was a missionary order, teaching and healing in Africa and South America. Their mother-house was in Turin, Italy. I had no interest in being a missionary but I didn't notice this at all. These nuns lived the simple life like St. Francis of Assisi: they got out there and mowed their own grass, chopped down trees on the wild wooded hills around them. They did not have private swimming pools and roller rinks as some American orders did but they recreated by singing, apple-picking and whatever simple joys they could create.

The summer before I entered, I took college credit classes through my longed-for university in a camp-like setting. My roommate was a wonderful friend but some kind of atheist or agnostic. This was a surprising experience for me. In addition, I dated all I could. With every guy I kept thinking, "This is my last kiss—forever!" It was just some kind of luck that kept me a virgin to the end of the summer.

By the time I came to the convent in the fall, I hardly knew if there was a God or not. But, I thought, "I committed to try this, and it will at least be an 'interesting experience' to add to my list of interesting life experiences."

However, one does not trifle with God. Once there, I found that everyone else took my "calling" seriously and took "God" seriously. I did not see an easy way out.

The general thinking about vocations to the religious life held another trap. It was felt that God calls us, not that we choose Him. It is, of course, a great honor to be called to this special life; sometimes nuns are called "brides of Christ." How could one say, 'No' if God himself were calling? If, after all, God is not calling one to this, God will make His will known by a sign: one might get sick, or one's parents might die and one must go home to take care of the siblings. I kept watching myself for sickness but nothing happened. No sign came that God did not want me here.

We were allowed to "consult" about our calling. Sister Angelica, a nun considered wise and holy, lived in a nearby house. I asked my superior if I could go talk with her. Mother Superior approved.

I went. Sister Angelica asked me, "Do you like to pray?" I answered truthfully, "Yes."

I loved to pray at that time, to have quiet time from emotional pressures, to try to find a clear path, asking for guidance from that Father and/or Son who I was told loved me so much.

"Do you want to spend your life serving God and helping other people?" she asked.

"Yes. Yes, I do," I answered. "That's exactly what I want to do with my life." "Then it sounds like you're called to be a nun," she told me.

You see, there was a general thought among Catholics at that time that lay people were called by God to populate the earth and carry on commerce. Anyone called to a life of prayer and service was being called to be a nun or priest or monk.

So I returned and continued to try to answer the call to be a nun. But life in the convent was hard for me. A severe curvature in my lower back has always made it difficult for me to stand on my feet for long and do ordinary physical activities. Young at the time, I just did whatever I had to do, but convent life was exhausting and painful. Also, I was only the third American to enter this order. No other girls entered at that time with me, so I was alone in my classes and training. This was especially difficult the second year when I had become a novice, wearing the habit, and spending most of every day alone with my novice mistress. The nuns were wonderful people but the life was hard, lonely, and tiring for me. I quietly passed my twenty-first birthday in the convent.

Every now and then I'd see another wise, holy person and ask if I could consult with them about my vocation. They would always ask the same kinds of questions: "Do you like to pray?" (Yes !...) Do you want to spend your life serving God and helping other people?(Yes !...) "Then, it seems you're called to be a nun."

At one point we were all doing a silent retreat. I asked if I could talk with the retreat master about my vocation. Of course this was approved and I went to him, trying again for more clarity in my endless feeling of confusion. This priest was experienced in counseling nuns. He just asked me one question: "Are you happy?" This was easy to answer. "No," I said. "Then you're not called to be a nun," the priest said simply.

I was out of there within twenty-four hours. I thought I was just obeying the priest. But as soon as I was home, I could feel my body relax and my spirit begin to lighten. I felt health and strength returning. Then it began to dawn on me. I had known all along that I did not have this vocation. Even my body knew. Something in me had kept me searching for the way out. I would never have stopped asking wise, holy people until I found one that said what I knew but could not say – this was not the life I was called to.

It would be many more years before I found my way through all the ideas that supported exterior obedience: to people, beliefs, practices, ideals, that did not give me strength to be true to myself. It was like swimming through underground channels trying to find an open path, a way that felt natural, joyful, and affirmed me. I did at last find my way up to the sunshine.

While I don't expect to be happy every day of my life, I've learned that a general sense of well-being is a sign of doing the right thing, and conversely, any situation that drains and pulls one down is a "sign from God" to change something. Never in my life was I taught this — that to be happy was a sign of doing the right thing.

For me, God the father and God the son did not save me but kept me ensnared, focused on them. It has been that quiet Holy Spirit who has been with me all along and still speaks inside my breast, affirming and nurturing me with the unfaltering dedication of a mother. She has guided me home.

Marti Matthews, friend to many, a mother and grand-mother, writer, spiritual explorer, counselor. Her book Pain: The Challenge and the Gift, *on the psychology and spirituality of suffering, was praised by Dr. Elisabeth Kubler Ross, Dr. Bernie Siegel, Dr. Norman Shealy, and Madeleine L'Engle. She was raised in western Michigan where she learned to love nature and music. She has lived in the Chicago area all her adult life, where her mind and friendships could expand limitlessly. She has been a member of the Religious Society of Friends since 1979, is now also a Unitarian, has studied Zen, Feminine Spirituality, Spiritualism, and the New Age teachings of "Seth"/ Jane Roberts, plus many other religions, theologies, and philosophies. For more Marti adventures, visit her blog: www.martiandfriendsexploretheuniverse.blogspot.com (marti_and_friends_explore_the_universe).*

A Trip to Freedom

LEIGH STIVERS

*May you be able to journey to that place in your soul where
there is great love, warmth, feeling and forgiveness.*
May this change you.
—John O'Donohue

My partner Ron and I were looking forward to our trip to Belize to celebrate my birthday in January 2010. We had the trip all planned out by March 2009. So I was excited. I began to read all about it and prepare myself.

That March, during one of my daily morning meditations, I saw a vision of a man approaching Ron and me. He said something; Ron replied. The man took offense. He pulled out a gun and pointed it at Ron. I quickly stepped in front of Ron, the man pulled the trigger, and I was killed.

"Spirit," I asked. "Is this the way it will happen or can I heal this before I go?"

I heard that I could heal the situation with forgiveness. It was Karmic, from a past life.

That day I committed to healing it and began

saying a prayer based on the Ho'oponopono, an ancient Hawaiian forgiveness practice:

I love you
I am sorry
Please forgive me
Thank you
Our Karma is done and complete.

This means: I love you for this opportunity in our lives to heal all that pulls us together. I am sorry for all the reasons and circumstances that pull us together in this life to heal this. Please forgive me for all that we left unfinished and for all we have not completed. Thank you for this opportunity to heal and move into a clean state of consciousness. Our Karma is done and complete.

I included all three of us in the forgiveness for we formed a unit of energy.

Right away, I received confirmation that my vision was not mere fantasy. My friend Eva Forrester stopped herself in mid-sentence of a phone call to ask, "You are not going to die before me, are you?"

Through tears I told her what Spirit had said and the words I affirmed throughout each day. She said she would also say prayers for me to heal the Karma.

That same week my best friend, Barbara, came in for a haircut at a salon where I'd served as a hairdresser for 48 years.

"You are not going to die soon, are you?" she asked.

Once more, through tears, I shared what Spirit had said and that I was in the process of healing this Karma. She promised to send me healing energy to help.

A day later, a woman who felt so close to me she called me brother, came for a haircut and said, "I have a feeling that you are going to die soon. Is that true?"

Again, I explained everything. I also explained that I did not want to include Ron in this process. This was my mission. I was committed to healing within, free from the interference of his energy—positive or negative.

I knew what I was doing was right for all concerned. If I needed to cry, I cried in private. I had no moments of worry, though. I'd lived a complete life and knew if it was my time, I would release the body with joy.

Finally at Thanksgiving, during meditation, as I heard, "It is complete," I felt a release.

Three times a day I began chanting: "Our Karma is done and complete." At least ten times a day I also chanted: "I love you for this opportunity to heal. I am sorry that it came this way. Please forgive me for this situation, and thank you for this opportunity to heal this."

By December I felt ready to replay the vision for the first time since that original meditation. I wanted to know it was done before experiencing it again. This time the vision came out differently.

Now I could tell Ron. "What?" he asked, after overhearing me on the phone, telling someone I had to talk to him. "What do you have to tell me?" I took him through the entire healing process, beginning, middle, and end.

"I'll cancel the trip if this is true!" he said. "Why didn't you tell me earlier?"

I explained that it was my job to handle this Karma through the help of Spirit. I knew within me that my steadfastness would complete this energy. After all, this was a healing process I had practiced for 25 years.

At last we were in Belize. One afternoon I forgot my diving suit. On the way to the store to buy a new one, a man with dreadlocks appeared out of the blue.

"Want some hash?" he asked.

"No thanks," I said.

"This is my religion!" he said.

"God bless you; practice your religion," I said, the words flowing from me. It was almost as if Spirit was talking.

He was so taken aback that he just stood there as we walked away. "That was the man I saw in my vision," I told Ron. "Now we are free!"

I continue to thank Spirit for this opportunity and gift. Anything life presents to us has an energy of completion within it. It is our job to focus on the gift behind a situation, to claim our spiritual power, to embrace the Grace of God. I am truly grateful to end the Karma that Ron and I created with this man from a former life. Thank you Spirit for all you do and how you bless us.

Leigh Stivers *has practiced spirituality for 46 years as a teacher, counselor, minister, speaker, mystic. His life is dedicated to service.*

Marco Prado

Aha! Moments Surround Me

MARCO PRADO

Life-changing moments manifest as we experience and learn from what's presented before our eyes!

I'd like to start from the beginning, I mean, from my early childhood in Brazil. When I was 9 years old, I knew for sure, with all my heart, that I'd like to be a Priest! I grew up in a household where my father was a Buddhist and my mom, a Medium with amazing healing hands to help anyone in pain or spiritually challenged.

As a good and humble kid, I went to church behind my father's back. My mom knew. She advised me to be careful of my father ever knowing. I was the best student in Sunday school. I helped the Priest on Palm Sunday to deliver the blessed Palms from house to house. I almost got caught by my parents who were driving near the church and saw a kid carrying large foliage. Luckily, they couldn't see my face. But my mom knew that was me, and distracted my father from that scene. Shortly after that, I had the chance to have my first communion, but I needed my parents' approval to go ahead. A big "NO" came from my father and the disappointment was beyond belief!

I had to mature 10 years in one day and let that dream go. I began by reflecting. How could I continue discovering more about spirituality and not be reprimanded? I realized I'd come to a crossroads with my previous karma. Too many past lives in cloisters. It was time to break that pattern. It was an amazing feeling. It's hard to think that at that age a kid would let go that easily. But I deeply understood within my soul. I felt a tremendous relief, as if my karma in that religious environment was ended for good, no resentment at all.

So, my first life-changing moment had begun. From that point on, I had an ongoing series of transformative moments that kept shaping my being and spirit.

Fortunately, my household was focused on healing and healthy living. Both my parents liked to help people. No wonder I came through their Spiritual DNA. I started becoming more involved in the channeling sessions that my parents held every Monday night at our house with a group of mediums. We also went to other peoples' houses for that. Growing up in Brazil, a Catholic country, this kind of living was quite secretive, but my parents were not closeted about it! They had friends who were gurus and channelers, a real group of first class healers. It was then that I got the hint of what I came here to be and do.

Today I share my ancestral knowledge and compassion for healing to whomever comes my way. I heal myself through their own process. I lived in New York City during 9/11. I went through the whole process of living two miles from Ground Zero and seeing the fall of one of the Twin Towers. It felt like the ground had opened up and we were all lost in that abyss with nowhere to go and nothing to hold onto.

I tried to offer my services as a Shiatsu practitioner to the surviving victims and their families through FEMA, the disaster relief operation. Shiatsu, which is Japanese for "finger pressure," is a hands on healing modality.

During a Shiatsu session, I use my inner wisdom to connect to the highest power within myself and the universe through touch.

But FEMA did not recognize Shiatsu or other

holistic work as disaster relief. Fortunately, I, and a group of others who were connected to The Olive Leaf, a Holistic Center in New York, got permission to offer our services as massage therapists.

For the first week, a military jeep picked us up at The Olive Leaf and took us through the barricades of the Piers to get to the tents. After that we reported directly to the site with proper IDs. This process went on 3 days a week for 3 months, after my regular job running a Shiatsu school.

Working with some of the family members of the victims was very rewarding. During my second evening shift, I was approached by a psychiatrist and a social worker to work with a young man of Indian descent. He was a waiter at Windows of the World, a restaurant at the top of the World Trade Center. On 9/11, he was supposed to work the morning shift. Only the night before, he asked a colleague to change his shift because he needed to go somewhere. That person ended up dying in his place.

The Indian man went into shock. He lost his speech and was under heavy surveillance by the nurses and doctors. Somehow, someone thought about bringing him for a massage. I was the only one doing Shiatsu and energy work. I was told he needed special attention. I did what I normally do. I focused on the mental and emotional aspects of his physical suffering. At one point, when he was face down on the massage table, I heard something he said. I then started asking him to speak a little louder. He burst out crying and released that emotional blockage. The doctor and social worker couldn't thank me enough for that breakthrough. From that point on, he could be helped by verbalizing his pain.

This experience brought me even closer to being of service when it is needed. This also helped me to detach from ego. It impacted the way I work today, with my heart open. Compassion speaks first and a nonjudgmental mind always comes into place. When we set the intention and work from the heart, everything happens!

Time passed. It was spring, March 2002. My mom, who was visiting from Brazil, came downtown with me so I could buy a new battery for my camcorder. The camera shop happened to be right across from Ground Zero, opposite the church that survived the whole ordeal.

Mom couldn't take her eyes off the site. I told her to stay close to the front door, not to wander down the block, because she didn't speak English.

After finishing my purchase, and testing my camera, I made my way to the front door, only to find her sobbing on the sidewalk.

Because she was a Medium, she was actually seeing and hearing what happened on 9/11. She described a horrific scene of people jumping and dying. They passed so suddenly, that they didn't know they were dead. They wanted to go home. Angels were trying to help them move on.

Mom and I moved closer to the site. I asked her to describe everything she saw while I recorded her testimony, the red light of the camera blinking. We were both in tears.

I was so excited, moved, and perplexed that I had to share the video with my sister the next day at a picnic on Long Island. We sat under a tree, talking. I played back the video. Nothing showed up! Absolutely nothing! I know that I had pressed Record when Mom was speaking. I know the red light had been on.

My sister and I both instantly got the message that whatever Mom saw and experienced wasn't to be exposed to the world. It was too soon. It was for us, so we could offer our healing.

Lots of prayers are still needed. Most people jumped and died in the air. I think these souls still await full understanding of what happened. On a spiritual level we need to help those souls who still await acceptance of their passing, to look for the light and allow themselves to be guided by the Angels. Most of them didn't want to leave the world because they were worried about their families.

There is much more between heaven and earth that our eyes can't see, but our hearts can feel! When it comes to the spiritual world, there are things that are not supposed to be shown, just felt at a deeper spiritual level. That's when we work with intention and an open heart.

Marco Prado is a Shiatsu practitioner who focuses on mind, body, and spirit integration. He is also a photographer that likes to integrate composition that comes from within, capturing the essence of life. His collection of curious moments is an organic process of working with images and apps that move as fast as his creativity does. This medium reflects the way he pays attention to life. With his restless creativity, a mobile device and regular camera in hand, he is able to make art wherever he goes. The combination of technology and emotion gives him the opportunity to be more intuitive in relation to color and composition. A lot of the themes in his work tend to be polar opposites. Find him at: www.envisionsforliving.com.

Awareness of Acupuncture for Your Soul

By entering into that space of wanting to learn and grow, even if it is painful to do so, we open up. Our emerging feelings, insights or experiences, like the gentle or not so gentle insertion of needles, allow our energy or chi to easily flow again.

Even so, sometimes there is no clear resolution, but simply a recognition of what is going on with us at the time and why we feel like we do. That's why Silence and Letting Go and Letting God is so important.

—Soonalyn Jacob

Keep quiet,

Listening, observing,

All with humility, acceptance, awareness and

You will know the next step.

It will unfold without your help.

It will unfold beautifully,

Even dramatically

If you truly let go

And Let God work on His own.

He knows how to do that, you know.

Miracles are just waiting for you to allow them to

Blossom like

Wild flowers,

Without fear,

Without wanting to take shelter

Or hide from your destiny.

Keep the image of a gentle colorful acupuncture

Treatment, releasing all your etheric bodies,

Clearing and strengthening,

Filling the void with JOY,

Laughter and fun for yourself and others.

—Rae

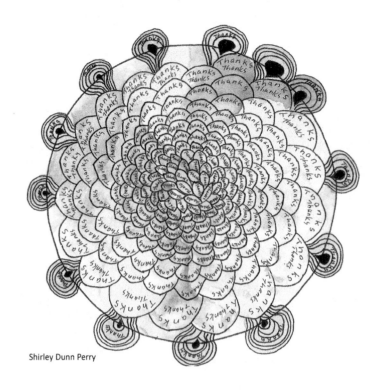

Shirley Dunn Perry

Blessed by Grace

SHIRLEY DUNN PERRY

As a child I loved Sunday School, the stories of heaven and the hope of becoming a good girl who would sit at the feet of Jesus. Anyone who could make a meal for hundreds out of a few loaves of bread was my hero. I needed a superhero to help me face poverty, physical abuse, and my mother's depression.

On the night my father died, and the church

63

youth director took me to his bed in the name of grief counseling, I became an adult. He did not force me when I refused physical penetration, even though my adolescent body pulsed with an excitement it had never known before. But God crashed and burned that night, as had Santa Claus years before, both leaving a trail of pain and tears. Somewhere in that complicated experience of my father's death, my budding sexuality, and the betrayal by my church leader, I branded myself as unforgivable.

Therapy in adulthood helped as I processed the experience. I could intellectually pardon myself, but the scar went deeper. One therapist advised me to observe adolescent girls, helping me to see that I had been a child who imagined herself an adult. Watching a gaggle of giggling and hormonally-dazed teenagers gave me perspective, yet I couldn't relate them to my fall from grace.

At age thirty-five, with one divorce behind me, I was in crisis again. I had moved with my five-year-old son from Canada to Massachusetts to live with my lover and his three children. The relationship was cracking, heavy under the weight of anger, jealousy, and stubbornness, as we attempted to blend families and find love.

Alone in my bedroom, I sobbed, my mind filled with rage and my body prepared for flight. I envisioned driving back across the border, defeated and angrier than I had been before I moved. Heartbroken, seeing no other way, I heard myself shout, "God help me."

Within a nanosecond, I was filled with peace, physically, emotionally, and spiritually. It was more potent than a rapid-acting intravenous sedative. I, and everything around me, was stilled. My mind, which had been spiraling into a black cavern, was empty. My tense body had gone limp. My spirit, with which I had little connection, seemed palpable, present, pulsating, soft and open. Had my eyes not been swollen and red from crying, I might have thought that my weeping had been a hallucination.

Somehow I was suspended above my circumstances, awake, aware, and full of a sense of wonder. Wonder of what? Love? Heaven? God? I felt alive in a new way, although I didn't know what had happened to me.

I never told anyone, and I struggle to write this as it's difficult to describe. I was full of awe, along with a lot of questions. Was I losing my mind? Might there be a benevolent, omnipotent Presence, available upon request? Might I be blessed with a Guardian Angel?

Not running away that day was a miracle. I had a habit of running. Now, thirty plus years later, after much hard work and many couples counselors, I am married to my beloved Jim for whom I'd left Canada for. Our family has grown and blossomed, leaving us to grow old together, and enjoy grandchildren.

I was changed forever on that day. More open to an energy force that is continually alert to all of my requests. Although my mind is unable to imagine what a Guardian Angel might be, I call upon the Divine Presence that flooded me with peace. I live in grace, secure that I am loved and protected.

Shirley Dunn Perry is an artist, poet, and nurse. Her passion is to empower others to express their creativity, and to align themselves with their heart's desires. She has a private practice which offers alternative approaches, such as painting and hands on energy work, for illness, pain, and life-imbalance. Explore her artwork at: http://artfiftytwo.com/. Email: ExpansiveVisions@Gmail.com Blog: https://shirleydunnperry.wordpress.com.

Milagros in Abundance

ANDREW GARTNER

Ghost white and weak, I sat across the table from Dr. Hazel Parcells, 92 years old, with twinkling blue eyes that sparkled like fragments of stars, dynamic red hair, and bright pink rouge on her cheeks. I was only 28 years old and 6'2" tall, yet I looked like a skeleton. In only three months, I'd dropped from 165 lbs. to 130 lbs.

How did this happen? I'd had an amazing dream job with George Lucas, married the love of my life, become father to my incredible adopted son Gabriel, and was accepted into the Master of Architecture program at Berkeley. All blessings unfolding simultaneously.

Then, when I was about to complete registration

for the graduate program, a sudden overwhelming feeling of sickness forced me to leave the registration office. I felt my lower body explode and ended up in the hospital with bleeding ulcers and a blood count of five. Thirteen is considered normal.

Everything had been so good, but even good stress can take its toll, especially when ignored. I prayed fervently, either to live a life of good health or to be led to a place on the other side of the veil where I could be of service.

Although alternative medicine was and is my first choice, I faithfully followed the instructions of the traditional Western medicine doctors. After no improvement, they said my only option was to operate and remove half my stomach! I refused, telling the doctors I would stop all Western medicine treatments and drugs. If I did that, they said, there was no guarantee I would live.

I took my chance. Back to fervent praying, acupuncture and chiropractic treatments. My acupuncturist told me about Dr. Hazel Parcells, a health and nutrition practitioner in Albuquerque that might help me. He suggested contacting her as soon as possible. What did I have to lose? Her next available appointment was three months away. I took it, wondering if I would live long enough to make the appointment. Or if she would!

Unable to work, my new son and wife and I left San Francisco to return to Santa Fe where we had family, where we met, where I felt a return to my soul's belonging. If I was going to die, this was the place to do it.

Finally the day of my appointment arrived. Dr. Parcells gave me the most penetrating expression. "You have traveled a long road to get to this place. You must travel the same road back to heal your body to the healthy place it once was. Are you prepared to make that journey?"

Her serious look transformed into a full smile with a contagious laugh that opened the skies of heaven for me. Her laugh was the start of my recovery. I felt safe in this woman's care.

After only three weeks of diligently following Dr. Parcells System of Scientific Living, the suffering and pain ended. I could eat again. I began to gain weight. Milagros in abundance! What more could I expect?

Miracles and magical moments flowed liked Niagara Falls. The Doctor's invitation for me and my wife to study with her launched a most privileged and fulfilling time of our lives. This was my remarkable gift from the Universe, the answer to my pleading prayer. For three years we studied with her, even filming a documentary about her life and work.

The Doctor taught us that every living thing is

made up of energy. She taught us to use a pendulum to check and record various energy fields around and within the body, mind, and spirit. This created a "road map" back to health.

She often referred to her System of Scientific Living as Simplified Kitchen Chemistry. The Doctor believed that everything you need to heal your body is in your kitchen cabinet. Food is your medicine. A huge challenge, but possible with her methodology.

Our passion today is actively sharing in our communities the Doctor's legacy with others, so they too can develop healthy nutritional practices, balance their bodies and allow Nature to do its work.

We have taught our children and now our grandchildren how to take responsibility for their lives and health using Parcells System of Scientific Living. I am eternally grateful for the gift of meeting, loving, learning and teaching about the Doctor. Doctor Hazel Parcells, 1889-1996, once honored as a Treasure of New Mexico, remains a priceless treasure in our family.

So many times I am asked for the secret of my longevity. I can assure you, there are no secrets. There is only the everyday practice of nature and the understanding of nature's laws.

—Dr. Hazel Parcells, on her 106th birthday

Andrew Gartner is trained in the field of Architecture. His hope is to offer people a place to find inspiration to live a happy life in body, mind, and spirit. Some of his projects include: Universal Studios Islands of Adventure, Lost Continent Adventure Park, Orlando, Florida, Into the West, a television movie for Dreamworks Production, and AmorePacific—"(Inner) Beauty Transforms the World"—Experiential Branding Centerin Seoul, South Korea. Thanks to teachers like Dr. Hazel Parcells, he gained a respect and understanding of the interconnection of all things in the environment and cosmos. He has applied these methodologies to the designs for three Montessori School campuses in which he has created experiential educational environments. Visit him at: www.gartnerdesignco.com.

I
am Love
and
I am
Everywhere!

Shirley Dunn Perry

73

Essny's Guiding Hand

MAUREEN MORALES

And those who were seen dancing were thought to be insane
by those who could not hear the music!
—Nietzsche

I first felt Essny's presence over my right shoulder.
She would come to me in quick flashes that grew
longer and stronger over time. I couldn't see her. I
couldn't touch her. I could just sense this strong and
loving presence that I knew was safe and I wasn't
afraid of it. At first she would just watch over me,
observing me. Her presence grew stronger in the
kitchen when I was cooking or even just talking about
food. I didn't know her name yet. I sensed that she was

a grandmother and some type of ethnicity. I knew that she wasn't mine, but was connected to me somehow. I have sensed other spiritual type presences in the past but had always found a way to dismiss them. I could tell that this spirit would be different. She had something to say or do but I had no idea what or how that was going to happen. I just knew I wasn't going to be able to ignore her. For the first time in my life, I was okay with that.

During the year that this presence began appearing to me, my friends and I also happened to be planning a large reunion for the hospital where we had all worked. The spirit came around very strongly when we met and lingered after the meetings. She also started flashing images of Kim, my close friend, who was also on the committee. The presence became stronger. She started to whisper ideas in my ear and gave me the feeling of knowing her opinion about the decisions we were making. A bit bossy, she injected herself into the planning crew whether we wanted her there or not. I finally mentioned it to the group. While a few thought I was a little crazy, Kim went home and told her mom. They knew right away that it was Essny, their Lebanese grandmother. Essny had come to both of them in the past. Once I heard the name, I knew that they were right; this spirit was Essny.

Once Essny was identified, the energy during her "appearances" became lighter. She was funnier and seemed happy that I had finally figured it out. She had played a little joke on me but now that I had solved the riddle, it was down to business. She swiftly promoted herself to Head Chef and placed herself in charge of the food for the Reunion Event. We were going to have plenty!

Although I still couldn't see her, I could sense a much clearer presence and image. She also began communicating with me more. She was even bossier, but still in a good way. She was in charge and we were going to do it her way and that was that. First order of business? We didn't have enough food. I didn't want to add more work. We were starting to get overwhelmed with the reunion approaching but Essny would not let go of it. We decided to add Machaca, a spicy beef dish, but that was not enough for Essny. She wanted LOTS of Machaca. She wanted a big pot. As I shopped for the food, Essny came around strong as ever and started moving my cart over to the meat section. I wanted to get 10 pounds of beef. She kept moving my hands to grab 2 more big hunks of beef. I kept grabbing the meat, putting it in the cart and then taking it out, saying, "No Essny, 10 pounds is enough." She just kept pushing for 30 pounds. The butcher probably thought I was crazy as I took the meat in and out of my cart over and over. We finally met in the middle and I walked out of there with 20 pounds of beef. Essny was smiling. I was proud that I had stood up to her and I think we both felt like we had won that argument.

That entire night before the reunion, Essny stayed up with me as I cooked her Machaca. Shredding the meat, grinding the chilies. She was right there. It was the closest we had ever been. The reunion ended up being magical. So much laughter and fun with old friends. So much love all around. Nobody wanted to leave. It lasted until the early hours of the next morning. After the event, Essny came to me again in a very intimate way.

She was tired, too. She was just like us, someone who had hosted a big party, worked hard, but had a great time. It was such a sweet side of her. We had pulled it off and she was as much a part of the team as anyone else. And of course we had plenty of food!

The day after the reunion, Essny started flashing images of Kim, but in a more concerning way. When I told Kim, she said yes, she needed to go to a doctor; she wasn't feeling like herself. Kim was diagnosed with kidney cancer and ultimately had a kidney removed. She was fine in the end. I think that was the original point of Essny coming to us. She just couldn't resist getting involved with the big party and all the fun. After Kim's surgery, Essny left for a long time. I really missed her.

About 6 months later, Essny showed up out of the blue in the middle of the supermarket. I was so excited, but she was rushed, like a busy mom just wanting to get the groceries done. She started leading my cart around, literally moving my hands to grab lemons, garlic and chicken. When we got home, I intended to find a recipe for these ingredients on the computer. Then I looked into the kitchen. For the first time, I actually "saw" Essny hovering around the food as if getting ready to cook. It was not a clear image but a mass of energy in rough form rather than just a presence. I realized I would not be needing a recipe. Essny guided me through a delicious broiled lemon garlic chicken recipe, step by step. Something I had never made before. Then she was gone again, quick as a flash.

Shortly afterwards, Essny came back, repeatedly flashing an image of a doctor in a white coat to me. I prefer to go to female doctors but she kept flashing an image of a male. I knew she wouldn't stop so I sat down at the computer and started looking through doctors in our network, image by image. All of a sudden, there he was—Essny's doctor. He was a Gastro Intestinal Specialist. That is what my husband used as his primary doctor so I figured it was okay.

The day of the appointment I became really concerned. I had lost a lot of people in my neighborhood to different cancers. Why was I there, anyway? I was only 47. Colonoscopies aren't recommended until age 50. I started making all kinds of excuses to leave. What was I going to tell this doctor? *I'm here because Essny made me come? She picked you off the computer? Oh and by the way, Essny is not alive?* I started having a little panic attack when Essny showed up and led me to a table with brochures on it. "I don't feel like reading right now," I argued with her. But she kept moving me toward the brochures. I picked one up and there was my doctor. He was from Lebanon! He was Lebanese, like Essny! She flashed, "It's going to be okay," and left.

The doctor scheduled me for a colonoscopy. I had 4 polyps, which he removed, and all was well.

Three years later, as I once again made Essny's Lemon Chicken, she showed up suddenly, softer and more distant. She started flashing images of the colonoscopy doctor, then Kim, then me, then the doc, me, Kim. I thought, *Oh gosh, here we go again* and started arguing with her that I didn't need a colonoscopy for another 5 years. I even checked with my husband, who is a nurse. But she kept flashing the images. I knew she wouldn't stop. So, I looked for the doctor on the computer again. I couldn't remember his name and the GI office had moved out of that facility. I started searching for female GI doctors but Essny kept flashing the same image of her Lebanese Doctor in the white coat. I kept telling her that he moved; I couldn't remember his name, but she just kept flashing. So, I started going through GI doctors on the computer and poof! There he was at his new office. I called. They said that I was actually supposed to come back in 3 years, not 5. It was 3 years to the month!

This time I had a carcinoid tumor in the ileum. A rare, slow-growing cancer that does not respond to chemotherapy or radiation. Most doctors do not check the ileum during a routine colonoscopy; this doctor did. Had Essny not handpicked this doctor, the mother tumor would not have been found and would have continued to multiply and slowly spread throughout my body.

The next few months were full of tests and scans to evaluate the extent of the cancer. I felt waves of fear and panic, not knowing what was to come. One day I was driving to Sedona with my husband when my beloved departed Aunts came to me amongst the beautiful scenery. Essny was behind them, reverent and quiet, as if she had taken a back seat. My Aunts, who had been Nuns in life, started singing the song, "Shepherd Me, Oh God." It was so calming and peaceful. Their singing opened up into a choir of angels coming perfectly from all directions, melting into the most beautiful sounds I had ever heard. "Shepherd me oh God, beyond my wants, beyond my fears . . . .from death into life . . . .from darkness to light." It calmed me throughout the remainder of the procedures. It allowed me to catch a little glimpse of heaven. I knew it was going to be okay. No matter what happened.

Today all is well. I had surgery and the tumor was removed. I go back for a colonoscopy in 3 years unless Essny says otherwise. My Lebanese Doctor visited me every day in the hospital even though I was technically not his patient. That is how wonderful he is. That is what a good Doctor Essny picked for me. I love you, Essny. You are a wonderful teacher and grandmother. You taught me how to open my heart and trust. You guided me through this journey and helped me to see what it's all about. Faith, family, friendship, and love. I will always make too much food for a party and eat more lemons in your honor. You are my special angel. Thank you.

Maureen Morales is a Pediatric Occupational Therapist *who currently works with special education students within rural Arizona school settings. She is a contributing author to the manual,* **Restorative Nursing for Long Term Care***(Cooper and Harrison Publications). Maureen has always had a bit of "the fey" and enjoys developing and understanding this gift. She also loves traveling, cooking, and spending time with her wonderful husband and three beautiful children in Phoenix, Arizona.*

Mary Holden

A Veil of Tulle, Titanium or Truth?

Mary L. Holden

Tulle in several layers, attached to a 1954 vintage beaded cap and wrapped in tissue, is stored in a yellowed cardboard box on the top shelf of my closet. My mother's own handwritten script is on the label: Frances Ellen Johnson, Wedding Veil. The veil's age made it fragile. Once, in deep grief after she died, I got this box out, unwrapped the veil and put it on my head. Although I longed for her arms, the tulle's embrace gave me some comfort.

As I looked at myself in the mirror, I thought about how Frances was more than a mother. She was a mentor, supporter, friend, teacher, kind neighbor, watchful companion. At her core, she was a champion of the unconditional love she experienced in a near-death experience while delivering her first child, a stillborn, who would have been my older brother.

In 2004 she died after 14 years living with an illness in which her body had been wrapped. I was both relieved and devastated. Her physical suffering ended, but I experienced grief like a ticking time bomb until it imploded.

Like the layers of tulle, other layers, unseen, separated me from my mother. It felt like they were made of titanium.

The hoop earrings I am wearing as I write this are titanium. Titanium is a strong, safe, medical grade metal appropriate for the day I chose to get pierced ear lobes at the age of 50, three and a half years after my mother's death. By then, I'd lost my fear of physical pain because the emotional pain after her death was worse than anything I'd ever experienced. I've always enjoyed good health and shied away from taking risks that could lead to even small amounts of discomfort. Even a stubbed toe brought me anger and fear of losing strength. Piercing my ears was a choice for pain—a pinpoint of hurt in order to heal, and then add beauty. Like Frances' veil, I wanted these earrings to be permanent symbols of the beauty of survival after loss.

Not believing I had the ability to communicate with unseen souls or guides, I spent four years asking the air (my supposed guides) for a significant dream with a message from my mother in her place-of-spirit. I kept records in a dream journal, but Frances never showed up and I was frustrated.

I decided to reach out to a psychic. Goldie, my father's mother used to say, "When you have a problem, don't go to a psychiatrist. Go to a psychic! They give you much better information." I found one in Los Angeles. An appointment was made for a Tuesday morning at 10, a telephone consultation.

On the prior Monday night, I had a vivid dream where my mother shows up looking young and vibrant. With her is a dog—a Beagle. The setting is at the house in which I'd grown up. We have a joy-filled visit, but her being with this breed of dog is a mystery because in real life we'd had a few mutts, a German Shepherd mix, a Dalmatian and a Husky— never a Beagle! Frances had been very close to the Husky. When he was euthanized, she was holding him in her lap, hugging him. Through tears, she told me how she felt the energy of his soul leave at the moment of death.

At the time of the appointment with this psychic, I was in the midst of a problem related to a business associate who had an unusual last name. The problem seemed unsolvable and hopeless. But I didn't plan to ask the psychic for help about it . . . I just wanted my mother!

I made the call and as soon as I introduced myself, the psychic said, "Before we get started, something very interesting happened just before the phone rang. I got a very vivid image of a Beagle. It was active, running around. It seemed excited about this call. Does that have any meaning to you?"

I was speechless. I don't even remember the rest of the call because I felt like a miracle had occurred.

But why did my mom bring a random dog with her in my dream? And how did she get it to also show up for the psychic?

Days went by and as both miracle and mystery sunk in, I felt that there was more to the story. I went to the Internet and googled, "Beagle Phoenix." The first thing that came up was a website for Beagle rescues. The uncommon last name of the president of the group was the same as the troublesome business associate. Same spelling.

Unusual? Yes, but a match was made in my mind. Frances knew I was suffering and that if I paid attention to symbols, she could get a message to me. In that moment, I knew that the problem with my associate would resolve with a good result . . . and it did . . . as if I too had been rescued.

Messages . . . symbols. These things carry much more weight than we know. I have always felt that the reason "dog" is "God" spelled backwards is because dogs, like God, give their owners unconditional love.

There is indeed a veil between the world we know as humans and the world of spirit. Is it made of titanium . . . or tulle?

In that moment, for me, it was made of titanium. For the psychic, tulle. Now I wonder if the veil is simply made of an all-new substance—resistance to its truth.

Mary L. Holden of Phoenix, AZ is a freelance editor and writer. She enjoys the "free" part of her job and uses the "lance" to improve words and sharpen clarity in communication. When the i in 'editor' meets the i in 'writer' we see eye-to-eye! Visit her at: www.marylholdeneditor.com (note the lower case 'l' between mary and holden).

Prayer is the most powerful force in the Universe—
And it is free—use it everyday.

—L. P. Hermes

The Pilot and the Prayer

TINA POWERS

Live life as though everything is rigged in your favor.
—Rumi

I always refer to my time as a television anchor as a past lifetime within this life. I spent more than a decade writing and telling stories about humanity. One day I would have the honor of meeting John Denver and the next I would be writing the story of a man who suddenly found himself homeless and was trying to find a shelter that would allow his dog to stay with him overnight. I learned everyone has a story and every story is important.

One of the disadvantages of news was that I found myself at the sights of many murders, hostage situations and plane crashes.

Over the years I developed a fear of flying. Mind you, I was not always afraid on every single flight. I even flew fine all over Israel and the Middle East. Go figure! But intense fears always came and went. Some said it was the feeling of being out-of-control. Other people thought perhaps I had seen too many terrible things and recorded them in my brain, making me fearful.

I was determined, however, not to stop flying or make my world smaller because I was afraid. I would get on a plane and hold on for dear life, especially, for some reason, while flying over water. I developed a ritual. First I'd ask for Saint Cupertino (the Saint for flying and pilots) to be on the flight. Then I'd down a shot of top shelf tequila. I was so sensitive I could also feel others' fears and take them on as my own. I did not realize this until I started consciously developing my intuitive skills. I always said a prayer before and while on the plane that all of the other passengers and myself would be delivered safely to our destination. Mostly though, I prayed that this sometimes paralyzing fear would be lifted.

There were many scary flights—one where I was thrown hard against the restroom wall because of an onset of severe turbulence. It got so bad that the flight attendant told me to sit on the floor and hold onto her leg so I would not be thrown into the front of the plane and seriously injured. In that moment I looked at the stewardess's eyes and saw complete peace while holding her leg. A funny, scary and yet poignant moment. Yet I always knew my prayers were answered and God was taking care of me. I always asked that if I was not supposed to get on a plane that I would be warned or protected. One night at LAX airport I witnessed an amazing answer to my prayer requests. As I was sitting with my family at the gate, our United Airlines flight was delayed. I had a feeling that we would not be flying home to Tucson that night. As we stood in line to board, the pilot all of a sudden walked off of the plane and announced to all of us in line that he was too tired to fly. He said he had been going since very, very early that morning and was exhausted and did not feel like he could safely fly us to our destination. I said a silent "thank you," so overwhelmed that my prayers had been answered that I blocked out the complaining of the other passengers.

As soon as I gained clarity, I could hear them talking about how inconvenient this was and how their schedules were ruined. How could he do this to them?

I turned to them and said, "I don't know about you, but I have always prayed that I never get on a flight where it is unsafe."

I thought to myself, 'Who cares about our schedule? We are alive! A pilot refused to fly. What a miracle!' I had never heard of that.

I shook the pilot's hand and so did some other grateful people, but those complaining would not relent. The pilot then took his briefcase and positioned it so he could use it as a chair. He sat there facing the people who were so angry at him. I watched him try to reason with them while he apologized for not being able to do his job at that time. I considered him a hero. He probably saved all of our lives by speaking his truth no matter what the fallout from the airline or customers.

I learned a lot in that moment. To speak my truth even if others don't agree. That some people are never going to hear the real truth in any situation because their own agenda gets in the way. But what I most learned is that there is a Higher Force looking out for us. When we pray and ask for protection and guidance, miracles can happen. I also felt the awe and gratefulness of my prayers being heard, as well as complete peace and protection. I witnessed a miracle and this is acupuncture for your soul. My soul.

It is **Tina Powers'** belief that we all have intuitive psychic gifts. Somewhere along the line we were told not to use them. It became more important what other people thought about us instead of what we thought and felt. Our value was dependent on others' viewpoints. She is hoping we will turn that concept around. Learning to trust ourselves, what we sense, and how we feel. Our psychic gifts are our inner compass. Our freedom. Recognizing the signs from the otherworld is uplifting, inspiring and freeing. In her book, **Reporting for the Other Side**, she writes about the transition from the television newsroom to reporting what she is hearing and seeing from the spirit world. On your journey, she hopes you learn to read the signs for yourself and know life does not end here on Earth. Visit: www.tinapowers.com.

Courtesy of Music for Health and Wholeness

Music of the Spheres

Suzanne Grosvenor

The shift into what became my life's work came about with no anticipation. Unexpectedly I began to feel, hear and sense experiences of life and all things in it as vibration, melody, rhythm, textures, harmony. No longer was music something external I could decide to do or not do—or how to do, as I had been able to all my life.

In a flash, the world transformed from what seemed solid to more liquid and changing. Beautiful, original melodies played in my head most all of the time, expressing and speaking of life itself at a depth I'd not known or anticipated in my years of music study or playing improvisationally.

When focusing on a person I would hear, feel and sense textures, sounds, melodies I could scarcely believe possible. Even the sound of a person's voice on the phone carried an extra, new dimension of subtlety, which could be nearly overwhelming. As we would speak about something mundane and practical, I was privy to an entire other layer of their being and vibration. It was almost as though the human voice emanated an ocean of energy and vibration, equipped with waves and tides, mist and sea air, and I was in the midst of it all.

The shift was completely unprecedented except for some early mystical experiences. Perceiving the world and life as vibration and music did not fit any previous preconceptions. This hearing a sort of musical accompaniment to everything, this experiencing the vibrational component to every life experience seemed comparable to awakening from a life in black and white, into a world explosively alive and overflowing in blazing color.

Were it not for music, I don't know how I could have expressed my new sense of life. And so I felt compelled to sit at the piano each day and transcribe the sound of life's music on paper. The music, confined to a page and now repeatable, held an interest unlike any music I'd written in my life, much less played. Piece after piece emerged in its entirety from the first note to last composed. Each piece was a tiny gem, capturing a moment, or reflection of a person I'd known for my entire life, or seen for a moment in a lecture. The music expressed in clear and definite language the nuances and subtleties of life, my perceptions and experience of my fellow human beings, of moments we shared and of the turning of seasons. There was no such thing as a piece of music that did not have a story to tell.

The music was not meant as art, but a language to accommodate my experience. As each piece completed, there was a sense of having stepped over a hurdle, of each piece being a stepping stone of my life, bringing awareness out into the open and allowing me to communicate my life more deeply, vividly, truthfully, meaningfully and succinctly.

When I released my first album of music that came directly from life, I did not yet know that I'd spend subsequent decades playing and composing the Music Portraits I heard emanating from people.

This began one evening as I listened to my friend Anthony tell a story. The music I heard while he waxed philosophical was not a reflection of his story, but of him and his psyche, his heart, how he felt and vibrated as he shared his life experience. That music launched my most rewarding work.

As I drove home, I replayed Anthony's music in my mind and transcribed it onto paper when I got there. I then recorded the music and gave him the cassette tape within a couple of days.

One week later Anthony called me, asking if I could transfer the music to a loop of tape that would play the song constantly. He'd been listening to the music as he carved in his workshop each day. While the music played, he felt safer and supported, encompassed in a familiar atmosphere, both comforting and reinforcing. He felt his creativity being turned on and more easily focused. He wanted to be able to hear the music continuously at his work table. Of course I made him the 8 minute tape loop.

The next time I visited Anthony, he couldn't stop asking questions about the music. What he really wanted was to sit next to me at the piano so I could instantly play the music as I heard it. I was not amenable at first. I had always listened to the music first, then written down each note, chord and harmony so I could capture every nuance. But he was insistent. Reluctantly, I agreed.

Anthony and I met very soon at my piano one afternoon. To my surprise, the music I heard and played for him flowed strongly though my awareness and fingers on the piano keys. Even more, it was as though the music was fueled by Anthony's presence. The music changed and morphed, picking up new momentum as he responded internally. It seemed as though the music was interactive.

Following each piece, Anthony shared what he'd experienced as I played. I marveled at what he said. The music brought him into a visionary state. As he traveled with the music, it triggered in him all manner of memories and impressions. The music spoke directly to him and, even more, reminded him of things of which he'd not been fully aware. I played this palpable field that I felt resonating, alive, around him. As I translated it to the piano, those same vibrations translated into the form of his feelings, thoughts and reflections on his life.

Anthony told me how, at one point, the music told him about things he needed to let go and talents and gifts he should keep cultivating.

The music, for Anthony, was a language that communicated direct information, just as it was for me. I was surprised. I had not anticipated that Anthony might suddenly resonate clearly, with impressions and insights awakening in him about his own nature.

He was so taken with his music session that he called several friends and urged them to call me, too, to come and have me play their Music Portraits.

This was just the beginning, a fulfillment of what had stirred inside me for all those years when I longed to know music as a direct language for communication. I had dropped out of music school because of the discontented feeling that music was being stuffed into me rather than encouraged out of me. I had failed my family and their never-ending support in the dream that I should become a concert pianist or college music professor. I felt I had failed myself in not realizing a university degree in music.

This journey that seemed to begin in failure has become whole and flourishing, thriving in an ongoing journey of discovery the likes of which I never imagined. Music continues taking me forward to this day, opening doors in awareness for myself and others.

Since that moment with Anthony, I have started teaching the method I discovered for Hearing Your Own Inner Music. It is not just for pianists, but instrumentalists and vocalists as well. The Music Portraits that I play for people are now recorded on CDs.

Music, I feel, is far more than an art form or entertainment. It is a grand and inexplicable language for describing in vibrational form, the subtleties of our consciousness through liquid, undulating terms. Music is a language of the heart and the spirit. When used sincerely for expressing what we sense of the moment, it opens us to greater depths in awareness of all that we are and can become. Without music, the unseen worlds within us may still be accessible. But with the help of music, what may have been difficult to realize, becomes easy and flowing.

There is a reason that music resonates so powerfully in our awareness, as it is a language for describing and evoking an entire dimension in our human experience.

Suzanne Grosvenor *is founder and director of Music for Health and Wholeness in Tucson, Arizona, USA. She provides custom Music Portraits known to support adults' and children's intuitive awareness, healing process and higher potential. She began performing her own music in recitals at age 8 and was guest piano soloist with a youth orchestra at age 10. In the 1980s she began hearing music "direct from life" and composed soundtracks for award-winning short films and video documentaries. She produced an album of piano compositions that became a favorite on radio stations around the US. Since then, her work has focused on Music Portrait Transformative Music Therapy in the form of private sessions and group gatherings (by Skype and phone as well as in person) and Music as Medicine CD releases. Find Suzanne at: musicforhealth. net and suzannegrosvenor.com.*

Dina Calvarese

Understood

HOLLY SACK

Seventh grade was a time of utter awkwardness. My lack of self-confidence and chubby body convinced me that it was a futile attempt, yet I smiled at the new cute boy in school, gazing at him from across the science room table. To my surprise, he smiled back. His name was Jeff. For the next six years, we dated on and off, becoming extremely close during our last two years of high school.

We loved each other very much, and in April of

my senior year, Mom asked me the question. "Hon, have you had sex yet?"

The intimacy Jeff and I shared hadn't included intercourse. "No," I answered, knowing that I longed for the experience.

With a kind heart, Mom looked deeply into my eyes and said, "Hon, it would be wonderful to have your first person be someone who respects you and treasures your body. I can see how much you love him and how much he loves you."

She could sense his tenderness and she felt that being with him would be a beautiful experience. And it was. Mom acted more as guide than mother. "If you would like, I can take you to get birth control pills."

Mom deeply trusted me and supported my independent thinking. Having my mother's permission to lose my virginity at age 17 meant that there was no judgment. She knew that this life-changing experience would stay in my heart forever. Mom gave me the freedom to do what I wanted and the permission to say no. My personal choices weren't always healthy ones, yet she knew that life acted as a training ground and opportunity to be true to myself.

Fast forward to 1976. A week before she died, I laid in the hospital bed with her. Pain medication helped put her at ease although her physical self continued to deteriorate. "Your father and I lived a hard life. We worked all the time and never stopped," she said. This was true. My parents not only worked at their own jobs, but after coming home, went to my uncle's tavern to help him and his business as well. She added, "Hol, you know how much I love you?" I answered yes. "If I could do it all over again, I don't know that I would have children."

I was speechless for a moment, as she gave me a toothless smile. I looked into her eyes and all I saw was kindness and love.

While it may seem like a hurtful comment for a mother to tell her daughter, I understood its significance. I heard her words loud and clear: I have a choice in this lifetime to be or not be a parent. She took a risk sharing it, yet I am sure that somewhere in that body of hers, she knew I would get it.

Thirty-nine years have passed. I don't have children. I do have gratitude, though. Every day Mom's encouraging words continue to carry me. Follow your intuition, not convention. Embrace your sensual self. Never take yourself too seriously. Be who you truly are.

Holly Sack is a certified black belt Nia instructor and has been teaching Nia in Tucson for the past 10 years. Her classes move people literally and figuratively with tenderness and high energy. Holly's insight and wisdom, along with life experiences facilitate openings for others to consciously discover themselves in movement. Nia is a movement class that combines 9 different forms of classical movement. It uses an amalgam of energizing and soulful music allowing for a loving connection to body, emotional peace, clarity of mind and an awakened spirit. She has been married to Rick for 25 years and knows her mother would have loved him.

Celebrating Acupuncture
for Your Soul Moments

When we can identify what we are feeling, we can consciously move our productive energy forward and up.

—Soonalyn Jacob

I am absorbed, enfolded,
Enclosed, encompassed,
Captured, and captivated,
Soothed, sung to and enveloped by the silence.
This is delicious, comforting, addictive.

Am I touching reality in this place
Or have I lost reality in this "other dimension?"
Or is this a bit of quantum space
Where we make our own reality?

Whatever it is —
For me it is healing, etheric endorphins!
What a privilege to be able to let go
And have the time — or take the time — To become
One with this Silence that is so alive and
Steaming with possibilities,
Information, and Caution Signs!
Crowded with beautiful Beings, Gentle voices,
Love.

It seems the air is pure oxygen —
Giving that exquisite sense of being fully alive,
Fully present.
The Earth School curriculum-agenda seems
Suspended during these splendid moments.

—Rae

Dan Jacob Jr.

Perfectly Aligned: The Little Blue Church on the Big Island

Tricia Davidson

Purpose.

My day began with a focus on lending support where I could, how I could — to a cause that mattered to me.

I was a few weeks into my training program, logging 3 to 4 miles a day, 3 to 4 days a week. Mine were small steps for a mammoth cause. Five months later,

I would walk 60 miles in Komen's 3-Day for the Cure event. I walked for many: my grandmother, neighbors, friends, and others in my life who were yet to be diagnosed. Each step was a step toward a cure and part of a journey toward greater fitness of my own body, mind, and spirit.

Observe.

I was reminded that so often while living everyday life, it is easy to become numb from habit.

It was late March 2005, shortly after sunrise. Four time zones away from home, I set out on my third day walking. I followed Ali'i Drive, a winding road that hugs Kona's west coast—the sunny side of Hawaii's Big Island. The air was island-fresh, so foreign from Minnesota's icy winter clime where I walked just a few days prior. My breaths were long and easy. They could be.

Breathe.

I couldn't have anticipated the rich benefit in store for me.

I had passed St. Peter's by the Sea several times, a tiny white clapboard church, trimmed in turquoise and capped by a blue tin roof. This particular hue of blue would most certainly be out of place on any building in the northern mainland; however, it was nothing but painterly perfect in the foreground of Hawaii's magical sun-kissed skies and rolling aqua waves.

Simple.

It was one of those lovely moments in life, where I was truly in the moment.

I was drawn to the church this morning. Approaching the front door, I was greeted by vibrant, fuchsia-colored, tissue-paper-thin bougainvillea blossoms, and the graceful waves of majestic palm fronds. St. Peter's is a Spartan building with a dozen pews that look as if they might have been converted wooden fruit crates dipped in melted, cerulean blue Crayola crayons. A simple wood pulpit and an etched glass window complete the sanctuary.

Alive and Aware.

There was so much to observe, clear colors, serene sounds. I was alert and curious about the detail in the natural beauty of just another day.

A view from the side of the church revealed a tiny building precariously perched upon a bed of black and grey lava rocks. These are the kinds of rocks that look as though they may have been dropped from another planet, with an almost extraterrestrial appearance. It was the unassuming brilliance of the unexpected. And I was open to it.

I entered St. Peter's, walked to the front pew, and peered out the window to the endless rows of waves.

Flow.

I breathed deeply, feeling an extraordinary, expansive connection in that moment.

Awash with warmth, tingling with chills—I was enlivened. Entirely. Immediately. The window's etching was perfectly in sync with the Hawaiian horizon. The view appeared eternal; the light stunning. It was the kind of magical "God light" that professional photographers can only hope for. The sound of the waves was mesmerizing. Hypnotic.

Spirit.

Something tapped my soul; triggered perspective; engaged a greater sense of appreciation.

A meaningful step in an ordinary day. The rare, connected presence of mind and body.

The gift of an unexpected moment.

Alignment.

Tricia Davidson *considers herself a life-long learner with a curious mind. Others might characterize Tricia by her many interests: nutrition and wellness advocate, wine enthusiast, design junkie, international traveler, music fan, aspiring yogi and gardener, photography buff, and puppy walker. Professionally, Tricia has established herself as a leading marketing communications consultant, with experience in multi-national agencies and as a founder of a world-class branding firm. Her advertising and design work has touched people's lives around the globe via businesses such as McDonald's, Bacardi, Coca-Cola, Sony, Susan G. Komen for the Cure, Amore Pacific, Water for People, and the Qatar Foundation. At the center of all, Tricia shares much of her energy with her family, whom she is also proud to call her friends. She lives with her husband and two children, whom she believes may be some of her best teachers. Through her journey, Tricia is intent on making a meaningful difference in all facets of her life.*

Marco Prado

Oneness at Samasati

Bonnie Kneller

Have joy and peace in the temple of your senses.
—John O' Donohue

As I savored the lushness and density of trees and greenery, we pulled up to a gate at the entrance of this remote mountainside yoga retreat center in Puerto Viejo, Costa Rica. I had never been to the Caribbean side of this incredibly beautiful and diverse coast. I was told that the gate was there to protect the land and the privacy of the guests. As I entered the main lodge I felt an immediate peace wash over me, both visually and viscerally. The sweet Barbara greeted me at the desk, explained the meal and yoga schedule and gave me a key to my room. My casita was on the top of the hill. It took 28 steps to reach it. I had no complaints. The view of the colorful and lush landscape and seaside village was worth every step.

As I walked around the property, I felt enveloped by nature and its indigenous primitive essence. The sounds of monkeys, birds, and insects singing and playing a symphony permeated this jungle wilderness. I felt as though I was listening to a chorus of animal beings communicating ancient wisdom and ritualistic sound patterns. I have traveled to many remote places on this planet but never felt this level of unconscious collectiveness as once described by the genius Carl Jung.

At my first yoga class in the meditation kiva, I found myself looking out the numerous windows of this round wooden dome. Trees whistled in the breeze, reflecting the sunlight streaming through. My body flowed through the asanas as I breathed in synchronicity with the sounds surrounding me.

I was prepared for the seclusion and tranquility of this sanctuary but not the amplification of natural sounds vibrating all through the night. Lying in my bed in this lovely casita I found myself vibrating to the constant chorus of cicadas singing and communicating with one another.

It made me think back to last summer, when I stayed at an old Gothic seminary on the upper west side of New York City. My room faced Broadway, a busy and noisy main street in Harlem. I couldn't sleep. Right outside my window was a bus stop. Every 15 minutes the bus pulled up and generated all kinds of mechanical sounds. I was a light sleeper, used to complete quiet in my own home in a private cul-de-sac. Increasingly agitated and annoyed by the constant noise, I had to move my room to the interior of the building before I got a good night's sleep. Would I have to repeat this experience in my jungle oasis? How could I drown out the incessant noise? I tried ear plugs and meditation but still was unable to fall into a deep slumber. Restless in bed, I began to think of all the teachings from my indigenous shamans and medicine people about tuning into and communicating with other animal species. I began questioning and doubting the validity of connecting vibrationally to these cicadas and being able to mutually coexist in this primitive landscape.

Finally, I decided to request that they be quiet for a few minutes so I could bask in silence and perhaps quiet my mind into an alpha state. Immediately after I respectfully made my request, they stopped.

There was complete silence for five minutes. I was astonished and relieved. Then the chorus resumed. Again I requested silence and the insect community reprieved. I was amazed. Somehow we were able to communicate and transcend the physical language barriers that existed in my mind. We had a reciprocal dialogue for about 30 minutes. I experienced the blissful oneness between human and animal—insect to be exact. Could this be possible? The cicada family and I communicating through some unseen world of language and connectedness? I found myself in a state of peace that I had never experienced to such fullness before in a natural surrounding so unknown and far away from home. Yet I felt as if I was home, one with all the beings that surrounded my little casita on the hilltop in the jungle of Puerta Viejo. I was washed over by the experience of interconnectedness that I have been searching for my whole life.

The symphony of the insect and animal world of this primitive land opened my mind to a collective consciousness I had only read or dreamed of most of my life. Awakened to a whole new dimension of communication, I was overwhelmed with gratitude. I felt a flush of understanding. I was and am not separate from the cicadas or any other life form. I realized in that moment in time on both a cellular and intellectual level the true meaning of oneness.

Bonnie Kneller was born and raised in Queens New York and later in Syosset LI, NY. She earned a BA in Psychology from the University of Colorado, Boulder in 1981. Bonnie earned her first Master's in Social Work from the Hunter Graduate School of Social Work in NYC in 1986 and her second Master's in School Guidance Counseling from University of Phoenix in 1999. She has had a private practice in Tucson for the last 23 years and previously in NY. She currently works at a large diverse inner city high school as a school social worker and has a passion for Diversity and the Arts. She has one son, 23, who is a musician and a stepdaughter, 31, who is married and lives and works in Southern California. Bonnie has practiced yoga and meditation for over 30 years and loves to spend time in her organic garden and hiking in the desert and mountains.

Mermaid Formula

Terry Duffy

On the way to Alaska, my husband, Andy, my eight year-old son, Dakota and I stopped to see our Aunt Judy and Uncle Richard outside of Seattle on Bainbridge Island. They had an incredible house, right on the edge of a cliff that overlooked the Puget Sound. Off in the foggy distance we could see city lights twinkling in Seattle and the illuminated Space Needle. Uncle Richard is one of the most amazing men I've ever met. He was the captain of a ship and an encyclopedia of endless information. He always had something new in store for us.

After we parked in their driveway, we passed their moss-covered fountain and Buddha in the entryway.

We hadn't even brought in our bags or hugged Aunt Judy, when Richard greeted us with, "Dakota, I need your help. Come down to the boat with me." Richard whisked Dakota down the steep edge of the cliff to where a rowboat was tethered.

Navigating one's way down the cliff felt like being in a Robinson Crusoe extreme sports show, as we leapt from one sporadic stepping stone to another, grabbed a vine, swung to the next level, and landed onto shells crushed into mud for better traction. I don't know which was more fun, the exhilarating fear of making it down to the beach or the view of sailboats, barges and cruise lines moving their fluid way onto their next destination of entertainment or commerce.

The small rowboat Richard led Dakota to looked like a toy on the open water. It could have been another one of the many finds that had landed on this beach from who-knows-where. "Dakota! Come on, jump in!" cried Richard in his Captain Bly's accent. "We have a treasure to gather!" We watched from the back yard as he handed the oars to Dakota.

Andy and I settled into a white cotton hammock that cast a grid on the green grass as the sun shined through. Judy sat by our side in the back yard and we could hear Richard and Dakota from down below even though we lost sight of them. They were gone for a good while and when we saw them again, Richard was rowing back. They returned tired, but excited. Dakota held up a huge rope to show us. We learned later that it was from a ship that Richard had spied a few days before, but couldn't retrieve or carry by himself. They both struggled to get the rope out of the small boat and drag it to the side of the cliff where it became the new handrail for one of the sections of the exciting descent to the beach.

Later that day after the new rope handrail had been installed, Dakota and I set out to test it. We screamed and laughed all the way down to the beach and then walked along the shore finding beautiful rocks and shells all along the way. When we saw a railroad tie tossed up on the beach we knew that Richard would find a good use for it as a landing to the stairway. We both ran over to check it out. Without a lot of discussion, we both bent down to wrap our hands around the very heavy wet railroad tie.

It was much heavier then either of us had suspected. Dakota lost his grip and the heavy wood beam slipped out of his hands and then out of mine to land with a thud on the top of my foot. So many things raced through my mind! Why hadn't I said that it was too heavy and we should just keep walking? Why had I not at least discussed a strategy, such as "Bend your knees," "Protect your back," or any of the other smart bits of advice that should have come out of a mother's mouth?

Now I watched my foot swell and turn black before my very eyes. Our trip to Alaska was ruined, I thought. That made me more obstinate. I was going to figure out how to make this right . . . but how?

I closed my eyes as Dakota sat next to me, asking how he could help. I started breathing deeply in order to try to deal with the pain and download information as to what I should do. We did not have cell phones with us. There was no way I was going to be able to walk back up the side of the cliff even with the new rope handrail. Without even knowing where the instructions came from, I asked Dakota to get me some seaweed from down in the water. While I sat with my hands on my foot doing energy work, Dakota brought back some seaweed. I then proceeded to dig a hole in which to put my foot. I put seaweed on top of it and layered sand on top of that.

I then was told to choose a large rock to weigh down the sand and seaweed. I knew that this wise child would pick the right rock and the perfect weight. It was not only the love a child has for their mother that was involved, but the way the earth guides us naturally to what we need that led Dakota to find the healing stone with the perfect energy for the job. Dakota handed me a smooth gray oval rock with a beautiful white lifeline wrapped all around it. We were always told as children that these rocks were wishing rocks and we would collect them and place them in our garden. I placed this perfectly weighted wishing rock gently on top of the sand that covered my injured foot. Our four hands went on top of that and we waited and breathed.

Why I was burying and layering my foot in just that way, I had no idea, but I was definitely being directed. We sat there for at least an hour. I had expected to pull my foot out and have it be black and blue and swollen since that's how it looked before I started the seaweed compress. When I pulled my foot out of the seaweed and sand, it was not black and it was barely swollen. As I spiraled my foot around in a circle both ways I realized that nothing was broken. I was going to be fine. I looked over at Dakota to see his eyes, huge and relieved. He couldn't believe that my foot was OK.

I love it when I feel that clear connection with some unseen force that's bigger than myself. What I love even more is the wide-eyed smile of a child witnessing this with their very own eyes, never to be forgotten.

Was this an old mermaid's formula that I had been given privy to or was it my own inner self, tapping into a flow of knowledge that is always there for us? I'm still not sure, but what I do know is that this experience made me doubt myself less and trust that inner voice to really know and always be there at the perfect time. This can happen at the oddest times or in the nick of time, but when it does I know I'm not alone.

As I stood on the back of a boat looking out at majestic whales in Alaska, I was so very grateful that I had taken the time to listen.

If you do not follow your messages, do not blame anyone else.

—Rae

Terry Duffy has owned her own graphic design business, Glyphics Design, since 1985. Terry graduated from Antioch University, San Francisco, with a degree in Alternative Health and Graphic Design with an emphasis in Photography in 1983. She studied with Dr. Jay Schear in Santa Fe, New Mexico and received her MT degree. She also worked and studied with Dr. Hazel Parcells, Albuquerque, NM for 10 years helping her to catalog and videotape her work, at the same time gaining a strong knowledge of the Parcells method. Her study of alternative/preventative health and graphic design has led her in many directions including exhibit design, book and magazine publishing and all forms of branding. A desire for clear communication has led her to be an educator that has curated shows, worked with scientists, writers and poets, trying new ways to communicate to people of all ages and walks of life. Terry is currently teaching ex-cons and foster care children anatomy and physiology through art. This class includes preventative care, encompassing Chinese Medicine, Homeopathy, Essential Oils and Massage. Terry is also a fine artist. To see more of her passion projects go to glyphicsdesign.com and terryduffyartstudio.com.

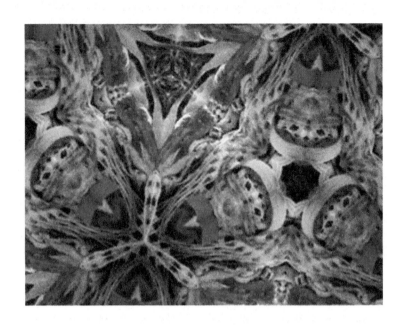

Queen of Sheba

Ann Capotosto

One day as a young child, I asked my dad about ESP. He just shook his head and said it was nonsense. Dad was a very intelligent man; I thought he knew everything. That was my first clue that he didn't because I knew there was something to it.

He did, however, redeem himself when he was annoyed because I wasn't moving quite fast enough for him with my chores.

"Who are you, the Queen of Sheba?"

'Actually, now that you mention it, yes, I am!' I thought. Fortunately Providence stuck a sock in my mouth so I only thought it, rather than said it. I had already learned to keep such thoughts to myself. I had no idea what it meant, no notions of reincarnation; it just felt right.

Twenty-five years later, I sat on the floor with my friend, Jean, who was wiped out from undergoing radiation for uterine cancer. I was filled with love and compassion for her present state of suffering. I desperately wanted to do something to help her. Hesitantly, I asked her to try something. "Please, just give me your hands." We sat there quietly. I concentrated on sending her energy. She felt it.

To this day, I am not sure what prompted me to do that. Somewhere, perhaps lodged in my cellular memory, I knew sending energy could help her. It took another fifteen years after this experience to find Universal White Time healing.

I was talking with a college friend who told me about a class she just took. As soon as she started to describe it, I knew this was what I had been waiting for. The first day of the first class I knew I had come home.

Universal White Time healing continues to be the most amazing thing I've ever done in my life. It is a powerful, yet gentle energy that is channeled through the practitioner and directed through the palms and/ or the third eye to the client. An Intelligent Force, it will go where it is most needed. Anyone can learn it. Universal White Time is very heart-centered. As it runs through the practitioner it actually energizes and gives healing to him/her as well. It works on the physical, emotional and spiritual planes. It can be done in person with a hands-on technique working in someone's field or aura, or it can be sent by distance with meditation. One can use it for self-healing as well. The more one uses it, the more powerful it becomes.

Although I'd felt at home with Universal White Time, the skeptical part of my upbringing was difficult to release completely. I never doubted the power of the energy I worked with, but struggled with my own ability to utilize it to its fullest potential. I used to angst before appointments, worrying that I would not bring enough to the table to satisfy my client. The anxiety was that much higher when it was a fellow energy worker.

Then one day the Universe sent me a client who was undergoing chemo for ovarian cancer. This was her second time around with it. She was out with her daughter and grandson when they decided to have their picnic lunch in the courtyard where my office is located on the most uncomfortable cement bench and table around, while the beach was only a few blocks away. She told me later that she'd walked around, checking the signs on each office door until she saw the bio I'd posted. She knew instantly that she'd found the person she wanted to work with through her recovery.

She is a very gifted energy healer herself and has been very psychic and open since childhood. I was blown away by her stories during our chats following the sessions. One day I did a series of gemstone layouts on her that I rarely use. (A great part of my healing practice is working with gemstone layouts. It is accepted that quartz crystal has a piezoelectric potential to make a constant and reliable frequency. That is why they were used in watch batteries and radios. Even though I know this to be true I am constantly amazed by the experiences my clients report— seeing colors, feeling movement, having emotional releases.)

The particular layout I used that day with my client connects a person with higher dimensional levels. I did not tell her beforehand and her report on what she saw and experienced almost brought me to tears. Her description matched all that I had learned with incredible detail. I was elated and humbled at the same time and it ultimately shifted me into a higher gear.

My whole journey has been a shifting of gears with many challenges along the way. We get strong influences from early childhood but we are not bound to them for life. Did my dad teach me to be skeptical, doubt myself or think critically? We make choices all along the way and how we choose to interpret information can help or hinder us. I asked his opinion and he told me what he believed to be true. Giving myself permission to break away from his belief was key to giving myself permission to grow as an individual. It didn't lessen my respect or love for him.

As significant as all these "Aha!" Moments were for me, none was more powerful than when I finally realized the most important step is unconditional love for oneself. Fully accepting one's human strengths and weaknesses are the key to unlocking the power within. Forgiveness of others' transgressions are important but forgiving yourself is the most freeing thing one can do. So much of our culture is based on blame and guilt. Once I figured out I could pick myself up and move forward with a newly learned lesson, doors flew open. As I relax into this sense of knowing and acceptance, more miracles are occurring. This truly is the shift of ages and we are the ones we have been waiting for.

Step into and claim your power. Awaken the god-spark we all carry.

Ann Capotosto is a practitioner of Universal White Time healing located in Redondo Beach, California where she lives with her husband and loving partner. She offers a wide range of services in person or by distance. Her continued education has brought her to the Board of Knowledge which is ancient knowledge only recently made available to us. Signs from the Board of Knowledge are tools to help open us up to greater enlightenment. As one grows, we all grow. For more information please go to her website: www. giftsfromtheuniverse.net.

Temporal Dowsing

SHARON KIRK

It was April 1999. Fear was rampant that the Y2K computer bug might strike at the turn of the twentieth century and shut down civilization as we knew it. I felt alarm of a different kind. I followed a sudden urge to call my Uncle Lyle, my mother's brother, who'd been married to my Aunt Zube for 60 years, not fully grasping it would be the collapse of civilization as my family knew it.

Lyle barely had the strength to answer the phone. I instantly contacted his neighbor to call 911. Fortunately, his neighbor was home. My handsome, world-traveled and progressive cardiologist uncle ended up in ICU.

I thought I could save him, but Lyle had already decided to leave this planet. After ICU, he refused rehab. A young doctor then took me aside, "When a 94-year-old man tells you he's going to die, listen to him." I believe that Angels' voices come through humans. Instead of sending Uncle Lyle home, I transferred him to a nursing home, where he went into Hospice. He had already signed all the necessary legal documents. He told the staff the amount of oxygen he needed (more than what they would have normally given). Then he laid down and waited to die.

For weeks as I sat with him, I imagined him as the Native American Elder who went into the woods to sit against a tree until the End. His home library had always been filled with books of the history of Native Americans in Arizona.

When I wasn't with him, I visited his wife, my Aunt Zube who lived in a locked-down Alzheimer's unit. Lyle had stopped visiting her because she would beg him to take her to their beautiful Tucson home with its 12 foot saguaro cacti, coveys of quail and gorgeous patio view of Mount Lemmon.

I swirled with questions. Considering Zube's dementia, was it safe for her to see Lyle? To attend his funeral? Could I manage her 24-hour medical crew at home? She had the money, but did I have the strength? Not even the trustee-assigned social worker could give me answers.

You might ask if I prayed for solutions. I had long given up on any traditional religious affiliations. Instead, I created an intention that members of my family would not suffer during the last days of their lives, and paid attention to what happened.

The perfect people began showing up for me out of the blue, the way I had been led to show up for Zube and Lyle. Even before I knew that empathic caretakers like me could become ill by absorbing a sick person's energies, help was on the way. A Reiki practitioner, an herbalist, other caretakers and a gemstone expert kept me healthy. I began shopping for higher quality foods at Trader Joe's and Wild Oats. I was guided to purchase gemstones to put in Lyle's room, as well as on his body. The hospice staff commented that his room was a peaceful space.

Zube did get to see Lyle before he died. Even though she didn't seem to know him, she stroked his head and was very sweet to him. At Lyle's funeral, her much-beloved neighbors supported her. When the hospice staff wheeled her into her home, she wept tears of joy as she looked at the fountain on her patio made of giant clam shells from their former home in the Philippines.

Less than a year later, she died in her bedroom. Her friends gathered once more in her family room, this time to celebrate her life. That day, one gardenia bloomed at the entrance to her house.

Marco Prado

There is no death, only a change of worlds.

—Chief Seattle's 1854 Oration

After settling Zube and Lyle's home estate, **Sharon Kirk** *spent four years in the White Mountains where she became the principal and teacher in a charter elementary school. She made long-lasting friendships in Show Low/Lakeside and Tucson and continued to study integrative medicine. She was present when her mother died peacefully in her home. For the past 12 years she has renovated her home to become a healthy sustainable systems environment; has been staff and event planner at Washington and Lee University; served on many sustainable education and local farm committees. She is on the Board for the Healthy Foods Coop.*

Shirley Dunn Perry

Rainbow Release

JENN MORGAN

My sisters and I decided to drop into Tucson for the surprise 60th of our dear cousin. The moment we arrived, Auntie knew I was "off." And off to her office we went. We chatted, she charted and then onto the table. Auntie practiced the Parcells System of Scientific Living. She'd studied with Dr. Hazel Parcells herself. Her pendulum circled and she made some notes. I didn't fully understand it. But I didn't need to. She cared about me. She wanted to help. I trusted her.

I expected a quick 20 minutes of relaxation laying

on what looked like a massage table under a soft colored light, then off to manicures and gift-shopping with the girls. What happened next I can't explain, but will never forget.

I got onto the table and tried to turn off the brain and settle in. I could feel the warmth of the lights and hear silence. Then that was it. I learned later that Auntie came in after that initial 20 minutes and told me to take my time and come out when I was ready.

Ready or not, I didn't come out until 2 1/2 hours later. What happened on the table, I still can't explain although I saw it all so clearly. I entered into a storm. The skies changed from a golden sunset to a deep blue to black. A lightning strike followed every thunderbolt. Colors filled my eyes, each one different but so intense. Pinks, blues, golds, white light. Tears streamed down my face at such an intensity I thought I was walking in the storm. I don't know how long this went on but I remember that with each breath the tears got bigger, the streams down my face got warmer and my heartbeat increased. Then it was done. The lightning stopped. The rain drops subsided to just random drops in the breeze.

I became quite fidgety on the table but initially couldn't open my eyes. I wanted to "wake up" but wasn't ready. I held no notion of time, and then I saw it. The most beautiful rainbow, each color so radiant so calming. These powerful rays were coming toward me. They continued until they were so close they blurred and surrounded me. And with that, my eyes opened. It was time. I was ready.

I rose from the table and walked out of the office, shocked to discover how long I had been there, shocked that the skies were clear and the land was dry. No rain, no storm, no rainbows for anyone else.

I missed the girls heading off to nails and lunch, but the new lightness, the openness to let go and forgive myself were all worth partying with chipped polish.

Jenn Morgan is a single mom working to balance two amazing children and a full time career. She is the behind-the-scenes mechanic blending linear processes and creative thinking to keep projects running smoothly in high gear. She finds strength and peace in family and close friends. Her mom and dad and aunt are her biggest role models. From all three, she learns dedication, patience and persistence.

The Necklace

SARAHNI (SUSAN) STUMPF

Until an event that occurred in my early 30s, I was a staunch agnostic materialist. Not in the sense of wanting more and more things, but in the sense of reality being determined by what our senses could experience. What I could see, hear, taste, smell, touch established my reality and I had no reason to question it, at least consciously. I had little interest in religion except as history lessons and had a particular disdain for that thing called "faith." I studied hard, worked hard, cultivated my personal discipline and will power and mostly succeeded in my undertakings. But, I admit in retrospect, to a deep but growing discontent. I recognize it now as a divine discontent, but back then it just felt like whatever I did just wasn't enough, wasn't satisfying. At work I wanted to be at home, at home I wanted to be at work. Vacations were great but so short-lived, I was always looking to the next thing. I funneled that power into continued study within my career field, always looking for ways to do my job better.

Then, within the time frame of one short phone call my world got rocked, and within 24 hours more my reality was shattered. My brother called to tell me that our parents' private plane had crashed into the deep ocean off the coast of Half Moon Bay, California. Nothing survived but Dad's flight case, his raincoat and one back seat. My parents were my and my husband's best friends. For many years they would fly over from Los Angeles to Tucson to spend a weekend a month with us. We would go camping, hiking or be tourists, just generally playing like kids. Then we'd return them to the airport and we would all become adults again for another month. It was a blow to have both dear parents and dear friends ripped away. That was a long and tearful night!

The following day I was on the portable phone with my sister while standing at my bathroom sink gathering things for a professional trip I was scheduled to take the next day. We were discussing whether or not I should cancel it to go to our parents' home instead, to gather with the others. Suddenly, I saw hanging from my necklace tree my mother's gold nugget necklace. This necklace was a large, single nugget in the shape of an anatomical heart. This was significant and precious to her as my father was an Internist/Cardiologist. Once he gave her this necklace, she never took it off. Her last visit to us had been 2 weeks earlier.

How had that necklace gotten there? My material

reality shattered. I got pushed through a door into a vast black hole. The door slammed and locked. I was forever changed.

I immediately donned that necklace and never took it off. I canceled my trip and instead flew 'home,' starting a trip into a series of synchronicities that continue to astonish me. They kept me in a constant state of questioning: What is going on here? Why is this happening? What am I supposed to do with it all? Who is in charge here? What is real? I was lost. I turned to the library and read voraciously anything I could find on death, precognition, reality, reality beyond reality. One dear and wise friend sent me a special book, *The Inner Life* by Charles Leadbeater. It was difficult slogging through, but deep within it there was a single statement: "What is on your mind at the moment of death, happens."

It answered how my mother sent (or brought) her gold nugget to me. It was that important to her that I have it, that I learn from their experience. It confirmed a reality beyond the material world. It confirmed that life doesn't end with death, just the physical body ends. It confirmed that those beings who had been my parents and my friends were not gone, just beyond my direct access to them. I paid attention to the rest of the book. It was like coming home, like remembering, not learning something new.

That moment contained the seeds of all the deep

understandings that would reshape my being. A Theosophical Society Study Group opened their hearts to me and grew closer than a family. They helped me get familiar with that which is beyond the senses. I came to understand a bit about the grand cycle of oneness into individuation and back into oneness; a great spiral of Be-ing of which we are all part and parcel and to which every experience contributes to the ever out flowing Be-ing.

Through Tibetan Buddhism, I grew to understand that what you see yourself giving (doing, saying, thinking) to others will come back to you. With this, you can create your future.

What future was I creating? My husband and I found ourselves in the position of the main administrators of a newly founded Buddhist university and retreat center in a remote area of southeastern Arizona, undertaking a 6 year course of training in the authentic, ancient secret teachings of the Gelukpa sect of Tibetan Buddhism. Our formal training culminated in a Great Retreat, 3 years, 3 months and 3 days in meditative seclusion.

Through that extraordinary adventure, I expanded into many levels of awareness. All of them are based upon a very clear understanding of the tenet: "We reap what we sow" and its many ramifications.

Everyone and everything is the soil within which we plant the seeds of kindness that grow in the garden of our world. Our day to day experiences, which we react to with more kindnesses. Everyday little helpfulnesses, pleasures given to others because we understand about seeds. Because we know their Divine all-potential, because we know our own Divine all-potential.

This is what I know 25 years later. In that moment, enveloped by the extraordinary kindness of finding my mother's necklace, all was yet to be.

Sarahni (Susan) Stumpf is retired from a career as a Physician Assistant and Acupuncturist. She left her work in medical care to pursue the wisdom through which people can find healing into ultimate happiness. She, with her husband, David, long time residents of Southern Arizona are enjoying the great outdoors year-round. They are both well-trained in the monastic teachings of Gelukpa Buddhism as well as in the Lam Rim, Stages of the Path to Enlightenment. They are eager to share what they have learned with others. Connect with her via email: healingstepsgroup@gmail.com.

Dina Calvarese

Grandma Rosa

KAREN CALLAN

Blunt, dramatic, and vocal, Grandma never veered from being honest. Oftentimes, her confident speaking voice and bold commentary put a legendary mark on the occasion. One never knew where or when the zinger would land. We just knew that it would. And memorable moments they became.

As a fifty-year yoga practitioner, Grandma made it her practice to live mindfully. Her colorful comments and enthusiastic nature lit up every conversation, yet her wisdom in meditation yielded a strong sense of her silent self as well. Both were happily passed down to me.

It's been fourteen years since Grandma passed away, yet I think of her daily. Every time I sit on the floor while playing games with my grandchildren or set out canvases and paints for them to be creative, I seek to embody Grandma. Every kiss and hug, clap and cheer, look and touch remind me of what is important in life. Each new experience fine tunes who I am and, ironically, the more I get to know myself, the closer my relationship is with Grandma.

She is my yoga teacher, my writing muse, my presentation audience, my resident chef, my walking companion, and my meditation partner. She sends messages and signs from the other side, usually in the form of song lyrics, neighbors' conversations, or public advertisements. When she passed, the song "Just In Time" played, sending me on the trajectory of a lifetime. Since then, whenever I hear the words *rose, Rosa,* or *just in time,* I know it's Grandma saying, "Ciao, bella. I'm here. I am always with you."

Like a good game of tag, when someone is given the gift of her story, they get to keep Grandma as well. I envision her traveling from person to person, offering her special talents of helping people fulfill their dreams, attain their goals, or release anything that is holding them back from reaching them. Imagining Grandma smiling as the song "Here's Rose" plays on my radio makes life fun. I see her throwing her arms out into the air, belting out the tune at the top of her lungs and making herself known. Not wanting to miss a sign, I listen carefully, paying attention to every nuance, every detail, every word. My sensors are always on high alert, waiting to catch the next joyful surprise. The more her presence is acknowledged, the more present she becomes.

I have been told by many people that after reading about Grandma Rosa or hearing her stories, she has helped them succeed in many ways. Being such a fantastic communicator here on Earth is possibly why she is so easy to hear from the other side. Plus, her knowledge of meditation most likely assisted her in this new position.

If you need help speaking up, ask Grandma. Widening your perspective, facing a fear, or taking the next big step? She'll be there. Writing a book or completing a project? She's your gal. If you want help in lightening up, adding more humor into your life or letting go of your resistance then look no further. "Bravo, bravo!" Her standing ovations are for you and they are infinite.

She was, and always will be the "Aha!" in my life. Grandma Rosa is acupuncture for my soul.

Karen Callan is an author, storyteller, and artist. Owner of Rosa Yoga since 2003, Karen is an E-RYT-500 registered yoga teacher who has taught classes, retreats and workshops across the country including The Yoga Alliance Conference, The Big Breathe, and The Sedona Yoga Festival. Laughter, listening to Broadway musicals and spending time on the floor with her grandchildren are some of her greatest pleasures. She and her husband Kelly share their time between homes in Tucson and Sedona, Arizona with their dogs Clay and Chloe. For more info about Karen's and her gifts visit: www.rosayoga.com.

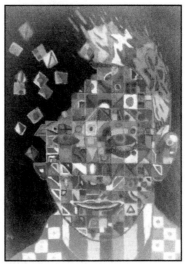

Morgan Olson

SO? WHY AM I HERE?
AND WHAT DO I DO NOW?

Nothing is all I hear!
"NOTHING" can be rich with information.

How about you?
What do you hear?
Why are you here?
Do you ever listen to the NOTHING—

The Silence?

Now what?

—Rae

Your Acupuncture for Your Soul Pages

When a great moment knocks on the door of your life, its sound is often no louder than the beating of your heart and it is very easy to miss it. To live a conscious life, we need to constantly refine our listening.

—Blaise Pascal

Liv Mundahl

Play with the following blank pages. They are ready for your exploration in words, thoughts, doodles. You don't have to write in complete sentences. Nobody has to understand what you're saying, but you. After you've run out of room, get a notebook of your own, or play on the computer. You'll be amazed by your own experiences. Turning to your own life again and again will offer illumination, laughter, support, and inspiration beyond your imaginings. Pick up a pen. Get ready for transformation.

Each of us carries the book of our lives inside our hearts.

—John O'Donohue

May you experience each day as a sacred gift woven around the heart of wonder

—John O'Donohue

Acupuncture for Your Soul

J. Lacson

Freedom & Flow to Continue the Dance of Life

Food for the Journey

Prepared for you by our Acupuncture Family.

Take what you want,

Leave the rest, and pass it on.

A prayer for all of Life's seasons:

Robe of Light

I clothe myself with a Robe of Light

Composed of the Love, Power, and Wisdom of God.

Not only for my own protection,

But so that all who see or come in contact with it,

Will be drawn to God and healed.

—Isabelle Hickey

Three Easy Ways to Feel Alive Right NOW

ANN CAPOTOSTO

1. Meditation is the best way to clear the mind. Start slowly. Five minutes is enough. Realize that there is no one way to meditate. I suggest using solfeggio tones from You Tube. Solfeggio tones are a 6 tone scale used in sacred music such as the Gregorian chants. 528 hz resonates with the heart chakra. Since everything in the universe is energy, dis-ease can be described as frequencies that are out of tune. Sound can be very healing. (For another take on the power of sound, see Suzanne Grosvenor's "Music of the Spheres.") After finding a meditation that feels soothing, sit or lie down in a quiet place. It doesn't matter which, just get comfortable. Roll your shoulders and your neck to relax. Shake your hands out if you feel the need. Take a few deep breaths and begin. Close your eyes and as much as you can, let all thoughts drift away. Do this everyday and gradually build up your time. As you grow more comfortable, you can pose a question to your guides, your angels, your

higher self. The answer may come in the form of a thought, a dream, a song. An animal may even appear in your dream or randomly cross your path. If it does, check out its totem message online or through books like *Animal Speak* by Ted Andrews. Trust yourself, you will know.

2. Another healing practice is the Hawaiian Ho'oponopono. (See Leigh Stivers' "A Trip to Freedom.") It is based on the belief that we are all part of a bigger collective of oneness. We know from physics that for every action there is a reaction. This is much the same idea. What I do affects you on some level. It is so simple to do and entails simply repeating 4 sentences. I LOVE YOU. I'M SORRY. PLEASE FORGIVE ME. THANK YOU. It doesn't matter if you do not believe it when you start, the longer you say it, the easier it becomes until it just flows. It doesn't even matter if you are the one who feels wronged. Be patient and trust. There is something magical about repeating it for 30 days. You can even do this to clear things with someone who has passed on.

3. I am a big believer in affirmations and have used different ones over the years. Just repeat them in the morning when you get up and in the evening before you go to bed. Do them anytime during the day.

I AM LOVED. I LOVE MYSELF. I AM LOVE. Dr Masuro Emoto, a Japanese author and researcher, studied the effect of words on water. He taped different words on jars of water. He then found a way to freeze the water and photograph individual drops. The water crystals labeled with words such as *beautiful, love, happiness* all created beautiful images, while words with negative connotations such as *dummy, hate, ugly* all created misshapen images. We are around 75% water when we are born. Think about the power the words we hear have on our being. Dr. Emoto showed that these inner messages can be changed. Affirmations are an easy way to reprogram yourself. Watching what you say about yourself and others even in jest is important. Just keep in mind the more loving your speech, the more loving you are.

WHEN UPROOTED — EXPOSED

LET GO

LET GO

LET GOD

LET GO

Be real about how you feel. Or do not feel. More options are available than death or defiance.

—Rae

Are the hardships of your life serving you, or are you a slave to a brutal taskmaster? Is your mind a prison or a prism? What I did on the outside of my life looks different from your life circumstances, perhaps, but the inside is identical at the core. We all have common ground where we "overlap." That sacred monastery of "overlap" is what I call, The Biggest Small Place in the world. It is a straight and narrow path, with enough room for all to traverse without pushing or shoving; all dangers come from the exterior of this sanctuary of serenity. Teresa of Avila might have called it the Interior Castle.

—Timothy G Cameron

The shadows play against the rocks.

The light and dark of the midday sun—like life!

The play of awareness and experience!

Dance with the Light

Step from shadow to sun

or

Stay stuck in shadow!

A PERSONAL CHOICE

—Rae

What I've learned . . . is that you should never let anyone extinguish your dreams, no matter how well intentioned those people may be. Pursue those dreams, aim high and make your own truths intentionally. Evaluate the advice you're given in the light of your own reality and don't accept it as absolute truth. After all, it's your life.

—Mara Aspinall
Biotechnology Industry Leader and Visionary

Imagine

Colorful acupuncture treatments

Traveling through all your energy bodies: mental,

Emotional, spiritual, physical.

Imagine

All no-longer-wanted or needed obstacles,

wounds

Being vaporized

Into a puff of cosmic colors.

Imagine

This clearing traveling through your personal

timeline.

Be discerning

This also vaporizes our excuses for not listening

to or

following our Soul's true path.

—Rae

Aha! Books and Websites to Light Your Path

Ann's Lights:
- *The Four Agreements,* Don Miguel Ruiz

Karen's Lights:
- *Loving What Is,* Byron Katie
- *Conversations With God* Series, Neale Donald Walsch
- *The Prophet,* Kahlil Gibran
- *Animal Spirit Guides,* Steven D. Farmer, PhD
- *Angel Numbers,* Doreen Virtue
- *Angel Wisdom—365 Meditations and Insights From the Heavens,* Terry Lynn Taylor & Mary Beth Crain

Leigh's Lights:
- *The Disappearance of the Universe,* Gary Renard
- All of Louise Hay's book and lectures
- *The Resurrection,* 1980 movie starring Ellen Bursty

Bonnie's Lights:

- *Oneness*, Rasha
- *The Power of Now and The New Earth*, Eckhart Toole
- *Illusions*, Richard Bach
- *The Alchemist*, Paulo Coelho
- *Siddhartha*, Herman Hesse
- *It's All in The Playing*, Shirley MacLaine
- *Eat, Pray, Love*, Elizabeth Gilbert

Terry's Light:

- *Journey Of Souls*, Michael Newton

Sharon's Lights:

- *Prescriptions for A Healthy House: A Practical Guide for Architects, Builders & Homeowners*, Paula Baker-Laporte, Erica Elliot and John Banta, 2001
- *Overwhelmed Work, Love, and Play When No One Has the Time*, Brigid Schulte, 2014
- *Zapped: Why your cell phone shouldn't be your alarm clock and 1,268 ways to outsmart the hazards of electronic pollution*, Dr. Ann Louise Gittleman, PhD, CNS
- *Healthy at Home: Get Well and Stay Well without Prescriptions*, Tieraona Low Dog, MD, 2014

- *Whole tones: the healing frequency music project,* Michael S. Tyrrell, 2015, wholetones.com

Rae's Lights:
- *Seeds of Contemplation,* Thomas Merton
- *The World Needs Old Ladies,* Gladys Taylor McGarey, MD, M.D.(H) and Eveline Dalley
- *The Physician Within You,* Gladys Taylor McGarey, MD, M.D.(H)
- Anything by authors Richard Rohr, Carolyn Myss, or John O'Donohue, Rumi, and Teresa of Avila
- *Healer: The Pioneer Nutritionist and Prophet,* Dr. Hazel Parcells, Joseph Dispenza
- *Live Better Longer, Parcells Center 7-Step Plan for Health and Longevity,* Joseph Dispenza
- Sara Calabro www.acutakehealth.com
- Danielle LaPorte www.daniellelaporte.com
- Timothy G Cameron, cameron.communications@ yahoo.com (watch for his forthcoming book)
- Soonalynn Jacob, www.spiralingupsolutions
- www.merylmartin.com
- www.thefoundationforlivingmedicine.org

Jan's Lights:

- Ten Thousand Whispers, Lynda Madden Dahl
- From Victim to Warrior, Leslee Morrison
- For inspiring short movies and documentaries: www.Karmatube.org
- To connect with the good that is happening all over the world: www.DailyGood.org

What It Means

The *soul* is the self, the "I" that inhabits the body and acts through it. Without the *soul*, the body is like a light bulb without electricity, a computer without the software, a space suit with no astronaut inside. (As defined by www.chabad.org).
The *soul* is spiritual and eternal.

Adventure—to engage in exciting activity, especially the exploration of unknown territory!

Acupuncture—adjusts and alters the body's energy flow into healthier patterns.

Divinity = God (Him or Her) = Spirit = All That Is = HigherPower = Universe = God-spark = Union.
There are as many names and as many unique views of the benevolent energy/being that is the essence of all life as there are people. We respect and honor them all in these pages.

Gratitude

It has been such fun and a great blessing to have these amazing, qualified Angels by my side in birthing

ACUPUNCTURE FOR YOUR SOUL!

LITERARY MIDWIFE/EDITOR

Jan Henrikson*

GODMOTHERS

Karen Callan, Shirley Dunn Perry, Diane Russell, Soonalyn Jacob, Kimberly Jacob, Betsy Grimes, Terry Duffy, Deborah Howard Jacob, Margaret Larsen, Lori Leavitt

GODFATHERS

Danny Jacob, Sr, John Morgan, Marco Prado, Randel Jacob, Leigh Stivers, Mike Fetrow, Ken Abdo

Karen Callan

*Bouquets of gratitude to our Literary Midwife, *Jan Henrikson* for her sparkling presence, and her keen, insightful, and gentle editing skills. Jan has been a major force in this book adventure by guiding and encouraging the writers who have so generously shared their personal life changing experiences. It has been a joyous journey filled with light, laughter, love and so much fun! Thank you, Jan!
You are loved and appreciated!

—Rae & The Acupuncture for Your Soul Family

For writing & editing projects contact Jan at
JanBookMuse444@gmail.com

Grand hugs and gratitude to my many patient and supportive family and friends, visible and non-visible!

and

An eternal thank you to each soul that has embraced, accepted, exposed and shared their soul's journey.

—Rae

About Rae

Rae's current passion is to pass on what she has learned to others who wish to expand their horizons. Her horizons really expanded when she began taking weeklong classes with Dr. Hazel Parcells, a pioneer in Energy Medicine and Nutrition. This privilege lasted from 1987 until 1995 when the Doctor died at 106. Her studies with Dr. Parcells launched an intriguing journey into energy, nutrition, color therapy and other ancient universal principles. Thinking "out of the box" is both fun and a great tool for not just "living longer but living better"! Today as an Inner Fitness consultant she shares Parcells System of Scientific Living and the healing energy of Color, Sound, Essences & More through her company, Raediance Unlimited.

Rae's forever passion has always been her six children, their spouses and thirteen FABULOUS grandchildren.

She lives in Tucson with her soul mate of 60 years and their spoiled, adorable dog, Smiles.

Visit: www.raedianceunlimited.com to contact Rae for consultations, workshops, lectures, gem elixir gifts, or just for fun, or find her on Facebook.

Want to share your inspirations, questions, or comments about the book?

Write: rae@acupunctureforyoursoul.com

Breeze

The breeze at dawn has secrets to tell you.

Don't go back to sleep.

You must ask for what you really want.

Don't go back to sleep.

People are going back and forth across

The doorsill where two worlds touch.

The door is round and open.

Don't go back to sleep.

—Rumi
13th Century

Randel Jacob

Thank you for joining our
Acupuncture for Your Soul
adventure.

We are so grateful!